PRAISE FOR *HOPE IN DISARRAY*

"More than an invitation, *Hope in Disarray* is a passionate
and personal summons to conscious and compassionate living.
Ranging through terrain as rough and varied as climate change,
racism, gun violence, and sexual abuse, this book challenges
readers to examine our comfortable certainties, imagine a more
just world, and take action to bring it into being."

—Dr. Laura Alary
writer, storyteller, and educator

"I turned the last page with a fresh infusion of inspiration
to live a life of compassionate, sustained action,
no matter how difficult the challenges."

—Brian D. McLaren
author of *The Great Spiritual Migration*

HOPE IN DISARRAY

Piecing
Our Lives
Together
in Faith

GRACE JI-SUN KIM

Foreword by Mitri Raheb | Afterword by Elizabeth Hinson-Hasty

the pilgrim press

since 1640

The Pilgrim Press, 700 Prospect Avenue East, Cleveland, Ohio 44115-1100
thepilgrimpress.com

Scripture quotations, unless otherwise noted, are from the New Revised Standard Version
of the Bible, © 1989 by the Division of Christian Education of the National Council of the
Churches of Christ in the United States of America, and are used by permission.
Changes have been made for inclusivity.

Published 2020

"Seeing Myself in the Eyes of a North Korean" by Grace Ji-Sun Kim is reprinted by
permission from the June 1, 2018, issue of the *Christian Century.* Copyright © 2018 by
the *Christian Century.*
"Indigenous People Teach Us about Climate Justice" by Grace Ji-Sun Kim is reprinted
by permission from the October 23, 2019, blog of the *World Council of Churches.*
Copyright © 2019.
"Becoming a Vulnerable Mother" by Grace Ji-Sun Kim is reprinted by permission from
the September 15, 2017, blog of *Feminist Studies in Religion.* Copyright © 2017.
"Mother Daughter Speak" by Grace Ji-Sun Kim is reprinted by permission from the
April 16, 2019, blog of *Feminist Studies in Religion.* Copyright © 2019.
"Uncovering Bill Cosby's Feet of Clay" by Grace Ji-Sun Kim is reprinted by permission
from the December 3, 2014, blog of *Feminist Studies in Religion.* Copyright © 2014.
"Memory Has No Statute of Limitations" by Grace Ji-Sun Kim is reprinted by permission
from the May 6, 2018, blog of *Feminist Studies in Religion.* Copyright © 2018.
"Western Domination and the Racialization of Beauty" by Grace Ji-Sun Kim is reprinted
by permission from the May 20, 2014, blog of *Feminist Studies in Religion.* Copyright © 2014.
"Longing for Peace on the Korean Peninsula" by Grace Ji-Sun Kim is reprinted by
permission from the January 22, 2019, blog of *Faith & Leadership.* Copyright © 2019.
"Removing the Burden of Shame" by Grace Ji-Sun Kim is reprinted by permission from
the October 15, 2018, blog of *Sojourners.* Copyright © 2018.
"Pope Francis Seeks to Reawaken the Church" by Grace Ji-Sun Kim is reprinted by
permission from the December 5, 2013, blog of *Good Faith Media.* Copyright © 2013.

Library of Congress Cataloging-in-Publication Data on file
LCCN: 2020934249
ISBN 978-0-8298-2114-7 (alk . paper)
ISBN 978-0-8298-2115-4 (ebook)

Printed on acid-free paper

21   22   23   24   25   5   4   3   2   1

For my beautiful niece,

Naomi Faith Bu

who inspires me and pushes me
beyond my limits
as I wrestle with hope.

CONTENTS

LIVING IN RELATIONSHIP

FOREWORD

Our world today is a mess. Politically speaking, the lessons learned in the aftermath of WWII seem to have been forgotten. International law, human rights, and the Geneva Conventions are being threatened by many world leaders and corporations. One need only look at the picture of the G20 Summit to see what kind of world leaders are governing today: from Trump in the United States, Modi in India, Xi Jinping in China, Putin in Russia, Bolsonaro in Brazil, Prince Salman in Saudi Arabia to Netanyahu in Israel, it requires nothing more than a glance to see that corruption lies close to the surface and that most of those leaders were brought to power by nationalists and right-wing conservative religious groups.

Environmentally speaking, creation is in agony. With climate change, global warming, and ecological vandalism, we are facing the worst environmental crises of our time. Islands in the Asia-Pacific region are slowly vanishing, climate disasters are hitting vulnerable regions of the world, large regions in Africa are being deserted, causing mass climate migration, and oceans are being polluted to an extent that is endangering all bio life and diversity. We humans have been encroaching on nature and wildlife for so long. Their space has kept shrinking. The coronavirus of 2020 came as a revenge to tell us: "If

you think you can keep doing this, we can lock you in as well."
Creation is groaning in pain, and though it is difficult to predict
where we are headed exactly, the future looks grim.

World religions are in no better place. They have often been co-
opted by the empire. Christian White-nationalism, Islamic Funda-
mentalism, Jewish Messianism, and Hindutvaism are on the rise.
Religion has been used to colonize rather than liberate people; its
patriarchal structures have been used to silence women rather than
empower them; and its race-based approach has made religious
services the most segregated hour at large.

Entering a new decade and closing another, we find ourselves
thrust us into a position shaped, corroded, and fortified by ceaseless
upheaval. It has led us to a state of division, outlined by the disruption of norms and traditional political parties, contrasted by the
intense social and economic fragmentation of societies devastated
by the effects of climate change; it's a place where bodies are traded
as commodities and social justice warriors confuse moral action for
whirlwinds of cyber-attacks.

All the efforts to cure our world seem to be too little and too
late. In such a context, it is easy to let those words of cynicism and
stories of unimaginable loss leave us without hope; it is easy to
believe that this world is lost and we need to await the one to come.
Only ultimate optimists might stick to the notion that change will
surely come and that justice will come for the deserved ones at the
end. Hope in this case is nothing but a delusion. Real hope has
nothing to do with delusion or illusion. Delusion is hope in costume,
and it allows people to keep observing the world indirectly through
a lens that falsely advantages us. It is a cheap hope that doesn't
reflect the real situation on the ground. It is an inferior hope that
shies away from confronting reality.

So how does one hope in times of disarray? How do we solve
the tension between hope and disarray? This is a highly philosoph-
ical question but an existential one as well. The Italian philosopher

and politician Antonio Gramsci, who was imprisoned by Mussolini's fascist regime, wrote in one of his letters, "The challenge of modernity is to live without illusions and without becoming disillusioned... I'm a pessimist because of intelligence, but an optimist because of will." Optimism, however, is not hope.

For Martin Luther, hope is the "sum of all Christian teaching." In Luther's thinking, hope has nothing to do with optimism. Optimism derives from optimum: the best that ultimately will come. For Luther this would have meant hoping in one's own merit. But merit leads ultimately to despair. In his commentary to Psalm 5, Luther described the Christian as "sinner in reality," yet "saint in hope." There is a saying attributed to Martin Luther, who was facing the empire of his time: "Even if I knew that the world is coming to an end tomorrow, I will still go out today into the garden and plant an apple tree." When facing a catastrophe, the only option left for the believer is not to run away, nor wait for the second coming, but to go out today to the society and act as if the brightest future is still ahead. Hope is a call to action today in spite of the grim outlook. What is important here, though, is that this action is not a reaction. A reaction would be to try to secure oneself, or to escape into a church to pray, or to meet to celebrate the countdown. Planting a tree is not something that will turn the world upside down, nor is it something that will change the course of history. Planting an apple tree is doing the ordinary, yet it is the context that makes it extraordinary. Planting a tree in a context like this might seem crazy. It doesn't make sense: a long-term investment when time is running out. What is crucial, however, is that the planting is done in the garden, in the society, in the public space.

In the Palestinian context there was a time when our people were optimistic, thinking that peace was coming, that freedom was around the corner, that liberation was dawning, and that we were approaching the end line. Many of our people were waiting for that moment to come. Yet, they waited in vain. Peace did not come. On the contrary, the situation got worse and worse. We realized that our struggle is not a sprint, but rather a long marathon. In a marathon, hope is the art to breath. It is the art to keep one resilient so as not to lose heart or sight of the goal. Hope is the power to keep focusing on the goal while taking small steps towards that future. Hope doesn't wait for change to come. Hope is vision in action today. Hope is living the reality and yet investing in a different one. The Jerusalemite prophet, Jeremiah, is the incarnation of this biblical hope. When his city was burned and the temple where he was serving was destroyed, hope seemed to be lost. Yet while the prophet Jeremiah was in prison, he asked a cousin to buy him a piece of land in Jerusalem. Jeremiah was able to imagine a future beyond the destruction around him. But that alone would not have been hope. Hope was deciding to invest in a city at a time when no sane person would so dare. Hope is what we do today. And only that, ultimately, counts tomorrow.

In this book, Grace Ji-Sun Kim wrestles with this same question of how people can hope when they are caught between hope and doom. How to hope when one realizes that one has little to say with regard to the state of things in the world. Grace doesn't shy away from these big questions but seeks to confront a life challenged by seeking meaning in an often meaningless context. Hope, for Grace, is putting desire into action. Hope is to fight, to rebuild, and to mobilize. As a woman, mother, wife, theologian, immigrant, Asian American, and member of a minority, Grace brings a unique perspective. As a South Korean, Grace brings a perspective from the global south into the theological landscape of the north. In her book, Dr. Kim deals with real situations implored for further exploration alongside her experienced theological insights. For Grace, hope is not an individual's dream, but rather a work of a coalition, an act of solidarity, a collective endeavor. Dr. Kim is reimagining the world, the church, and the culture in their intersectionality, interconnectedness, and interdependence.

Although *Hope in Disarray* reveals how hope is essential for discussing the political, the book is established on a spiritual framework that grounds us in a time defined by materialism and self-service. The different sections function as daily devotionals as well as a base for Sunday school classes. The different chapters journey through as a spiritual guide, passing through the church year from Advent through Christmas, Lent to Pentecost, and beyond. The questions at the end of each section are valuable for reflection and discussion. *Hope in Disarray* is a formula for an authentic faith anchored in Jesus of Nazareth, who was born and died under occupation, bringing liberation into our world. It is this hope that can lead us through troubled times and towards a future marked with justice and a culture of peace.

Rev. Dr. Mitri Raheb
Bethlehem, Palestine

ACKNOWLEDGMENTS

I wrote this book to provide words that would walk along with those seeking spirituality and hope in their lives. With continual meditation, I thought of the reader's faith as a guide, flickering past the lines of enrichment and provocation as words were shaped, erased, and recreated. Faith, and strength in one's faith, is the reason why I share my thoughts of hope—to address the ways in which our relationship with God can be not only supported but intensified during times of our suffering and our hopelessness. In the process of redefining my own hopes, I found myself drawing closer to another understanding—that the reader's faith, used to give meaning to the book and the writing process, was really mine. Our faith is united on this front. It is the reason why this journey of writing to seek hope in a world of disarray gives me the very hope for the troubled world that I write about. For this, I am eternally grateful to the process and to all of those who helped me along the way. The ideas in this book are not only a reflection of myself, but a patchwork of many minds who have graced me with their influence.

I begin by thanking Rachel Hackenberg, my editor at Pilgrim Press, for her uncompromising vision, guiding me graciously to the completion of this book. I also thank the wonderful staff at Pilgrim

Press who went beyond all expectations to help this book realize its highest potential.

I want to thank my friend Dr. Mitri Raheb for his kind foreword. His work never ceases to inspire, and he gives the gift of hope when I most need it. I am ever grateful for his piece and relish his generous contribution. I am also thankful to Dr. Elizabeth Hinson-Hasty for her gracious afterword. She is not only a brilliant fellow Presbyterian minister, but also a friend who has grown to serve the church, challenge its teachings, and provide unconditional compassion in her work. For her words, I am always thankful.

To my research assistant, Bruce Marold, I express my deep gratitude for his excellent editing work. His assistance was immeasurable as he patiently and consistently worked alongside me to elucidate the articulation of my thoughts and theology. I extend my gratitude to my student assistants, Leigh Waltz and Caroline Morris, who provided fruitful work and insights on the manuscript. My friend Mark Koenig read portions of the book and offered vital feedback and suggestions. Naomi Faith Bu absorbed herself in the composition of the text. Her dedicated time and keenly modern perspective gave new light to this book.

I cannot go without thanking my family for their support. As my children, Theodore, Elisabeth, and Joshua, continue to grow into inspiring and galvanizing individuals, they have encouraged me in my work and my writing. I thank them for their abiding love, comfort, understanding, and advocacy during this journey. My daughter left warm cups of tea by my bedside when she sensed me becoming unnerved, while my two sons offered me back rubs after extended hours sitting at my laptop. I am thankful to my husband, Perry, who lovingly took the burdens of extra housework and chauffeuring the kids so I would be able to meet deadlines. His steadfast compassion and sacrifice kept me and our family afloat. To my sister Karen and her family, thank you for opening your home and sustaining me with a place to rest and share meals in the years of my writing.

I acknowledge my mother, who passed away from cancer much too early for her time, but who left me with the invaluable, eternal seed of faith, which has bloomed since her death and provided fulfillment in my life. I am thankful to my father, who drove our family to countless churches across denominations, communities, and borders, thus shaping the person I longed to become. Their imprints are everywhere in this book. I honor both of them, as they dedicated themselves to establishing the foundation for my theological journey, exploration, and imagination.

This wonderful community of family and friends cannot be thanked deeply enough. Their support inspires within me the courage to write theology that brings love, joy, and empowerment to all.

INTRODUCTION

We hope for many things in our lives. From mere minutes that transcend us from one moment to the next, to the course of years and decades, to the approaching era of a new generation, we all possess a set of expectations imposed on a time that has yet to come. Amongst the many things we have hoped for in our lives, we have all likely shared one hope some time ago: to be picked up and held. An instinct of any child, this early desire springs out from our nature—our natural desire to be seen, touched, tended to, and guarded in our physical connection to another being. As we mature in life, we continue to reiterate this hope, crying out and reaching our arms up wondering if we can grab hold for just long enough to feel satisfied. We reach for love, dreams, attention, status, and the fantasy of an ideal future, merely holding onto a perfect destiny not knowing if it will ever be realized.

When we hope, we are taking a certain risk into our hands. This risk is a quiet virtue, an expectation towards something that does not belong in the past or present, or in the material world at all. It is an expectation towards the unknown distance ahead of us, where nothing is seen and nothing is possessed. Despite our blind desire to create a future that may not exist, we continue to reach out and call for it because we believe in it nonetheless.

So then we must ask, why do we hope? How can we better understand hope and its preservation in our lives? First, we must understand that we are investing in something to come. In our finiteness, we surrender to the reality of time bound in the physical world and the coming spiritual world. Early Christians depicted hope as an anchor, confident stability to be fixed onto the shore of the afterlife. Ask yourself, where do your anchors truly lie? Are they settled into the artifice of schedules and ambitions and rules you have made for yourself? Are they being lost in the desires of daily life? We are urged not only to investigate our anchors, but, as Christians, to walk towards the one at the very edge of our worldly existence.

Hope is anchored to the very presence of God, the "inner place" that dwells without discernment. The anchor is not in the very place where the ship is, rather a place removed, a far greater, holier place.

The places of focus in my life are family, social justice, and God. These are the most important things to me. As they exist in the complicated confusion that is our lives, these realms of focus exist in nuance and seldom bob out in clarity. When I think of my family, I think of my children—the lives they have lived and the lives I hope remain long ahead of them; I think of my parents, and my mother who is not here anymore; I think of my husband, my chosen partner with whom I have shared the better half of my life and will continue to do so. When I think about family, I am always hopeful, but the abscess of worry and fear also lingers in the back of my mind. It creeps in despite my optimism, as such hope relies on certain order, which does not exist.

I know this is the case for the majority of us. It seems that we are always in the midst of this duality, caught in the limbo of hope and doom because of the inevitable loss, pain, and suffering we endure. That is what comprises life. Many of us live in a state of shock or grievance because of these pains, growing cynical as we age and endure more loss. It seems that finding a semblance of joy or peace may be a remarkable outcome of our hopes being realized.

It is why we get up in the morning, it is why we go to work, it is why we try and do things we do not want to do—to reach a goal and to see our efforts and sacrifices yield return. However, true joy and peace do not come from our dreams being realized, and they certainly do not come from outcome. In fact, it is the opposite.

Romans 15:13 states, "May the God of hope fill you with all joy and peace in believing, so that you may abound in hope through the power of the Holy Spirit." This verse exhibits a perfect condition where we are filled with joy, lifted from all our sorrow, and where we are filled with peace, lifted from our fear and animosity. This condition describes a blessed state of being, one where we hope to be in joy and peace—yet it tells us that this is not the pinnacle of our character development. Rather, we go on to "abound in hope," meaning that joy and peace are merely the prerequisites to thriving in hope. This establishes a hierarchy where hope is the final end, because hope is what saves us. It is what anchors us in our malady and disorder. The hope we maintain changes us and becomes us, though it is another side of ourselves; it is a self that looks far past what we are in the moment and, instead, to where the anchor is.

You may ask yourself, where am I? I always find myself asking this question, wondering what it means to occupy my current space and body. Personally, this space is a woman, a mother, a wife, a theologian, an immigrant, an Asian American, and a minority. Admittedly, these categorical demographics are ways that I, and others, have come to define myself and even fall back on. In preserving these titles, I have sought to find clarity in my identity and, thus, in my experiences. But is there a way to neatly explain and understand experiences through these titles? No. That's my simple answer.

Being an immigrant informs my experience as a woman, which informs my work as a theologian and thus as a Christian, just as being Asian American informs my experience of being a minority. But all these channels of influence have no direction; they ebb and flow every which way simultaneously. I see how the multitudes of titles have brought about the sexism and racism that permeate our society at large. Because I grew up in a time and place of less social awareness, nearly all my early experiences have been wrought with explicit prejudice. I continue to bear the internal wounds of this experience, and whatever titles you bear have likely also brought you trouble. Living through these skins, we are shown a world of constant social, economic, religious, and political afflictions with little say in how it is. We grow weary of them, tired of them, accept them to be a part of our nature. Most of us give in to these issues, believing that their inevitability is enough cause to become apathetic. But this is the easy route. It is the road traveled. It is one that is self-fulfilling, temporary, and straightforward. Living with hope is much more of a challenge. It begs you, despite your suffering, to confront life with all the dimensions of its complicated truth—to confront the truth that life does not end in vain. Living with hope is to uphold expectations for goodness and the ultimate revelation of the Son of God.

The theological and spiritual reflections found in this book reflect my own meanderings of hope and faith. They are reflections on seeking God in the midst of turbulence, inequality, pain, suffering, happiness, and love.

This book can be used as an individual spiritual devotional book or it can be used in a group discussion setting. Each reflection begins with a biblical passage and ends with discussion questions designed for further reflection and conversation. We will move through discussions on pertinent world issues to contextualize how our faith and hope will work through them: living in the church, living in culture, living in relationship will be ventured through in the intersection of fear and abiding hope. You may choose to read this as a book of medi-tations in response to the challenges of our world through theological-spiritual journaling. This approach can allow us to contextualize the disarray of world issues within our own individual states of being.

When we become aware that God is present in all of life, in all our difficulties, we begin to live with hope. As life pours down sadness, struggle, and unbearable pain, we try to seek God and live in hope. In difficult times, we can only run on hope. When our world seems as "hopeless" and broken as it is, hope gives us the purpose to go seek out the meaning and the necessity of pain in our plight for justice. We have nothing to cling to but our belief that faith will sustain us. I have made this my daily task, and I urge you to do the same. Faith and hope work together to remind us of our shared humanity and to strengthen us as one in our fight for social justice.

Hope is a confidence that has altered my worldview dictated by fear to one that acknowledges peril as necessary for justness. It grows day by day. I live with an enduring devotion to this sentiment: that the longer I live, the more adversity I face and the more patience I cultivate for a growing hope.

Figure out what to hope for: this is the least we can do in our lives. The most we can do is to live inside it, to reside forever within our hope, to take our final breath and find assurance in not knowing if such hope was fulfilled, but that it was the hope itself that fulfilled us each waking day. As I search for God's presence in the world and in my own personal life, I recognize that my story is not mine alone; it becomes the community's story, the world's story, of suffering, love, and faith. In our unified experience of life and the suffering that comes with it, I offer some of my own understandings of discovering and living with hope to build divine union between you, your future, and God.

HOPE IN DISARRAY

LIVING IN THE CHURCH

Practicing empathy is central to our lives as human beings. We hold onto our positions of virtue and compassion with a kind of nobility that is most prevalent in religious institutions. As Christians, we frequently infuse our discourse and personal identities with such notions, enacting the importance of caring for our neighbors and finding forgiveness, mercy, and love for those who may seem to be undeserving beneficiaries: our enemies or our opposers. Yet, when we think of others in this light, we have to consider the reality that we are not the emancipators of the spiritually lost or the physically ailing, but, rather, equal partners. We Christians have to release our judgment and self-righteousness that has been misappropriated to oppress.

Forward progress is vital, but we cannot turn a blind eye to our history. We must always remember and honor our past. Our past is an ugly one, filled with atrocities arisen from grossly imbalanced institutions of power. It is integral that we recognize this part of our history in order to understand how previous mistakes and scriptural misinterpretations can evade us in the future. It has not escaped us today. We continue to live in the hundreds of years of past manipulated understanding. Thus, in our rapid and labored pace of cultural and religious change, we must look towards the most progressive state of theology: intersectionality.

This kind of theology reveals that there is not one comfortable right answer, and that the space of the church must allow for the expanding room of complex and diverse understanding. It is vast and all-encompassing. For this reason, intersectional theology feels less comfortable and wrung of painless clarity. It is a sprawled, messy, and opaque window. It embraces the full scope of contradictions and blemishes of the conflicting human experience. That is the very beauty of it. That is the very trueness of it.

We need to embrace this challenge in order to understand the true profundity of Christianity in the changing world. It is not just an empowering approach that is intended to uplift minorities or oppressed groups, but an essential perspective of the opposing dominant groups that possess the economic, political, and social power to shift the global worldview and make an impactful difference to us, the Christians of the world. With the perspective of intersectionality, embrace the newness and the intricate development of ideas that will give us greater hope for a more loving world.

WAITING IN HOPE
Advent

> The true light, which enlightens everyone, was coming into
> the world. He was in the world, and the world came into
> being through him; yet the world did not know him. He
> came to what was his own, and his own people did not
> accept him. But to all who received him, who believed in his
> name, he gave power to become children of God, who were
> born, not of blood or of the will of the flesh or of the will of
> man, but of God. And the Word became flesh and lived
> among us, and we have seen his glory, the glory as of a
> father's only son, full of grace and truth.
>
> *—John 1:9–14*

Advent is a coming into place, a coming into being, a coming into
view; an arrival; the coming of Christ into the world. This is how
advent is defined. It is an undefined time before an occurrence, a
time of waiting, a time to contemplate what is to come and ponder
the meaning of the change that it will bring.

When we look to nature, we are in constant anticipation of the
next arrival: the rainfall after thickening clouds, the emerging crack
on the egg's shell, the retreat of the tide after the surge, the full rise

of a new day. These normal yet sublime periods before "arrival" are time spent in the limbo of alteration. They are not a moment of stillness or nothingness, because what occurs amidst the change is an active movement of new transition. But during these moments of transition, do you ever ponder the arrival of the familiar? Do you ever stop to fully recognize the unquestionable and fated process of change?

Children experience change in wonder. I remember my oldest son walking out into the rain for the first time, touching it, jumping in it, and tasting it with an open mouth and a head tilted up to the sky. Afterwards, every time he stepped outside, he would eagerly watch for the clouds to gray in hope for more rain and in hope for new, thrilling revelation. This story reminds me how children actively experience and practice one thing that many adults have all but forgotten in the face of waiting: hope. Children are more effectual in the process of anticipation, as they are actually looking forward in excitement. Every new change brings them an alloy of joy, fear, excitement, and heightened consciousness, filling their spirit and providing us a second chance to re-experience the mundane as marvel. Reconnecting with the hope of a child can reawaken us to joyful anticipation.

Think of this anticipation in the context of the Advent season, a season of waiting for a new arrival. The commercial excess that much of the Western world undergoes during this time as well as the emotions of family communion, holiday frivolity, and the approach of a new secular year provide plenty of distractions that can keep us from maintaining the central focus of Advent. Much surrounds us to divert our attention from the seminal event of biblical revolution: the arrival of Christ, the second coming of Christ, or the *parousia*. Advent hinges upon preparing for a celebration of Jesus's birth and, ultimately, his return. Advent is posited on what is to come. It looks towards the birth of Jesus at Christmas and towards the second coming of Christ. Hence, it looks towards the future in at least two ways. When we look towards the future, even a future in God's hands, we live in hope.

Putting the future into context currently, we may feel at a loss with the quickened pace. Personally, as I age every new change that occurs is attuned to a heightened, new kind of speed, a globalized, hyperaware, self-improving, polarizing, and coalescing kind of speed. The changes we have experienced have given those of us in the developed world more connection and more isolation, more freedom and more limitations, more solutions and more problems. These things in their own form are arrivals and departures—fundamental changes. In confrontation with these daunting changes of the world comes a medley of reactions: fear, despair, cynicism, ignorance, indifference, vigilance, calm, action, protest, and kinship.

Advent reminds us that all these changes await us, transforming how we act and react in the new world. While we wait in anticipation, in the rapid speed of the adapting world, do not let fear take hold and stifle our hope.

Advent is a monumental, distinctive season when we are invited to spread the joy of waiting. We are to reaffirm the truth that we are not just celebrating the birth of Jesus, but anticipating his second coming. We hope in the knowledge that we are not just awaiting an infinitely loving God, but we are also being awaited by God.

The beginning of Advent is a period of awaiting; it is a period of hope in purest form. A new liturgical year is inaugurated, and with it comes the novelty of God and corporeal nativity. The period is a direct response for our doubtful or uneasy disposition during newness, as Advent is the gospel of anti-fear. If fear forces us to the ground, God lifts us up; if pessimism pushes our heads down, Jesus turns our gazes towards the heavens from which he will emerge again. He will come, and we will not live in fear because we are not children of fear but the children of God.

During Advent and any period of anticipation/waiting/expectation and change, stand up and look to the sky. Open up to your neighbors and embrace the consolation that comes with transformation. Experience the gracious, galvanizing anticipation of waiting, as we stand by with God's emboldening hope.

Reflection

1. When have you waited for something to arrive? What did you do to make the time meaningful?

2. What spiritual disciplines and practices do you use to wait in the Advent season?

3. What have you learned during your Advent waiting that you can apply in other times of waiting?

THE HOPE OF CHRISTMAS

> But God proves his love for us in that while
> we still were sinners Christ died for us.
>
> —*Romans 5:8*

In a world filled with heartache, death, and pain, God offers us hope. It is not hope that comes with ease but hope mustered during the most painful times in our lives, rooted in the life, death, and resurrection of Jesus. It is hope that emerges from our darkest moments and brings us out onto the other side; it is hope that allows ourselves to experience life's greatest pains and willingly accept its bleak beauty because it enriches our life and our humanity.

We know death to be a profound certainty of life. Even with that knowledge, when someone we love dies, our whole being is shaken and veered off its familiar course. It can be the most overwhelming, confounding, infuriating, and crushing experience to lose someone before their time. Often, we come to question everything when a life is lost because it demands that we try and make sense of the life we still have and how we are to go on without the presence of the lost other. We try and rebuild our life, but our efforts to closely regain what we once had prove to be a hollow endeavor. Because, despite it all, life cannot be what it once was.

I return to this idea time and time again when I think of my mother's death. As I reflect on her passing after ten years have gone by, I feel lucky to have known she was going to die ahead of time. I had time to prepare for it.

When my mother was sixty-three, she started to cough. It seemed to be a harmless cough, a little cold—only this cold didn't seem to go away. After months of coughing, my sister finally convinced our mother to go see a doctor. What the doctor found at the walk-in clinic was unusual, and he sent her to a specialist. After weeks of examinations, scans, and waiting, we received a diagnosis: stage four lung cancer. Six months to live.

I remember that phone call from my sister like it was yesterday. I can still recount where I was and how my ears began to ring, my vision was bleached, and every thought simultaneously evaded and crossed my mind. How was life going to be taken from my mother, who had lived so healthily, so honestly, all her life? They must be wrong. They must be wrong, they must be; six months is not right, she must have more time; she's strong, she's healthy, they have to be wrong; she's going to beat it; she's going to survive.

At the time of her diagnosis, my mother was living in Toronto while I was living with my family in the United States. Bearing the pain of my mother's illness and life expectancy was even more difficult because of the miles that separated us. While she was beginning to endure the drain of chemotherapy, radiation, and Chinese medicine, I could only see her for intermittent periods. At each visit, I saw the woman I knew and loved diminish as she became taken over by illness. During the quiet and breathless drives to visit my mother, I always felt like I wouldn't make it in time, and that I would just be another minute away from missing her death. In the last few weeks of her life, the doctors moved her from the hospital into hospice care. Somehow in the midst of it all, I felt that my mother could be cured of this terrible disease. I did not fully allow myself to accept the fact that she was reaching her death.

But the doctors ended up being right. Exactly six months later, she passed away. It was two weeks after Christmas.

Before Christmas is Advent, a time of loving and peaceful waiting as we prepare to celebrate Christmas. As we are waiting for the birth of Jesus, joy and hope fill the spirit of Advent. But that year, neither Advent nor Christmas brought love and peace or joy and hope to me. The season was restless and devastating. I was overtaken by hopelessness because of the imminent death that my mother faced. After Christmas, my mother's death brought additional pain and sorrow. A time that was meant to celebrate the miracle of Jesus' coming and life became a time of grieving, and ultimately the most difficult loss of my life.

In that experience, I know that I am not alone. Many people understand Advent and Christmas to be a landmark time of loss, tragedy, pain, and suffering. Our melancholy is further fed by the commercial "joy" of the season, where we find ourselves even more broken amongst the collective cheer of the holiday season.

Yet we remember that the hope of Christ's birth is found first in Christ's death and resurrection. Our faith reminds us that through life's greatest tragedies, pains, and most devastating losses we find meaning in our suffering through Christ.

We will grieve our losses. Our grief may be long and bitter. Grief is a price of love. Yet as we grieve, we may discover that even in our most profound sorrow and suffering, we find light; we find beauty; we find gratitude; we find hope. We learn that while we will always mourn the losses of those we loved the most, we will also celebrate their lives, their presence, and their being as a miraculous gift.

Christ came into the world as a little baby. A baby who embodies the joy, peace, and hope of being alive. The world that Christ entered was not democratic and free; rather, it was a world that knew occupation and domination under the Roman Empire. Poverty, patriarchy, and strict laws created divisions based on gender, age, and religious status. Illness and infectious disease pervaded the world, and most died young while even fewer made it past their middle age without serious ailment. This world from the distant past is not far from the world we find ourselves in today.

I began to lose my mother during Advent. She died two weeks after Christmas. I see this now not as a tragedy of Christmas, but as a sublime indication that her life's end aligned with the time of Christ's birth and that, through it all, the pain of watching her go was a gracious reminder of life's miracle: death is not the final act.

Through God's love we were sent his Son. Christ came into this dark world to give us light and love and a hope that can break through the pinnacles of darkness, illness, and even death. This is why I celebrate Advent. This is why I celebrate Christmas. This is why I celebrate my mother's life. As I continue to reflect on my mother's death, I am reminded of hope, for it was during the season Christ was born.

Reflection

1. Life is full of tradegies. What are some of your deepest pains?

2. How have you overcome loss and pain? How have other people cared for you when you have experienced loss and pain?

3. How might we care for family, friends, and others who may be experiencing loss and pain?

CHURCH LIFE

But the hour is coming, and is now here, when the true
worshipers will worship the Father in spirit and truth, for the
Father seeks such as these to worship him. God is spirit, and
those who worship him must worship in spirit and truth.

—John 4:23–24

Since I was young, I have always woken early on Sunday mornings
and anticipated the day. Church presented itself as the convenient
hybrid between a community center and free English classes, and
my father was ever inclined to take advantage of such a resource
after immigrating from Korea. My sister and I became enveloped in
a burgeoning church schedule: on Wednesday nights we had Bible
study at a Baptist Church, Friday nights we had fellowship at the
Missionary Alliance Church, Sunday mornings were for Sunday
school at another Baptist Church, Sunday afternoons we attended
our regular Korean Church, and then later in the evening we made
our way to a different Baptist Church for Sunday night worship.
Back in those days, my whole life was centered around church. Due
to my poor English, I didn't have much of a social life at school, so
the knowledge that I would be able to play with other kids on a
loaded schedule was a saving source of kinship.

Undoubtedly, church was an essential part of my upbringing. This is why I frequently get frustrated with my children. They grew up attending church once a week. On Sundays when I wake them up they often plead with me not to go. When I try to wake up my youngest to go to church, he rolls and moans around in his bed for as long as he can. He pretends to sleep and continues to ignore me. Then, at a certain point of annoyance, I usually start making more noise and aggressively raise the blinds, strip him of his covers, and command him once more to wake up and get ready for church. He'll huff out, "Seriously, AGAIN?"

Then I'll yell back, "What do you mean AGAIN? This is the first time this week!"

While it both irritates and disappoints me, I can sympathize with my son. I had thought the same way on countless occasions when I was pulled against my will to go to church. I know that this is a shared experience for children, but it is also one that afflicts adults. As a minister, I have seen many people who were once regular faces attend less and less frequently, until finally years go by without seeing them at all.

There are a multitude of reasons why someone may not return to church. Most often, it is self-appointed. You may justify it to yourself, meditating between reasons and excuses as to why you don't need to go. What is the point? I am already secure in my faith. What is the benefit of leaving home to go to a physical space? Most of us have likely considered such questions. Since technology has made nearly every service more accessible, convenient, expedient, and customizable, the necessity for church attendance is being put in question like it never has been before. Church services are taped and put online, and now with the advent of livestreaming, we are able to watch services in real time. We may be glimpsing into a promising future of the church through the democratized access of church services for the unable and the curious, yet we cannot deny that it stifles the agency to engage in a physical space of worship and the natural fellowship that follows. Thus, we must remind ourselves of the virtue and essentialism of attending service.

The Bible reminds us that we must not neglect "our meeting together, as is the habit of some, but encouraging one another" (Hebrews 10:25). There is power in coalition, community, and togetherness, especially with other believers who can strengthen your faith as you do theirs. We all long for meaningful connections in our lives. Perhaps those we have with members of our church can be some of the most significant ones, because unlike most friends who pass through our social circles during different periods of our lives, the kinship we share with companions at church endures despite distance and despite passed time. God has given us a gift in calling us to gather with one another for church. It deeply fulfills something within us to do life with another, as we embolden and revitalize one another to be more involved in each other's lives. While there is much to gain from other sources of Christian education through books, podcasts, livestreams, and TV, nothing can replace our physical church for the education that comes with being part of a Christian community. We can grow more together than we can alone.

The faith community is a large factor in maintaining our spiritual health. We need to hear what others have to say as we grow in faith and as we encourage one another in the process. The church is the optimal place for children and youth to begin their spiritual journeys; they are immersed with the like-minded at the foot of life's path to understanding the gospel. While young children and teens can have fellowship with other Christians around their age, adults can form strong friendships at a time when so many feel they cannot form new friendships or maintain them. Church can become a special place where people of all races, ethnicities, classes, abilities, sexual orientations, and gender identities can come together in commitment, to worship, serve, and support one another. An intersectional church recognizes that people experience multiple intersecting realms that come together and reshape our lives.

In our journey as Christians we are not called to do it alone. We need one another. The church was designed from its origin to function as the living body of Christ on earth after Jesus' resurrection. The apostle Paul tells us, "for as in one body we have many members, and not all the members have the same function, so we, who are many, are one body in Christ, and individually we are members of one another. We have gifts that differ according to the grace given to us, prophecy, in proportion to faith" (Romans 12:4–6).

We need to be in regular fellowship with a breadth of believers so that we may benefit from their spiritual gifts and ultimately offer our spiritual gifts to them and the body of Christ. As we share our gifts with one another, the congregation we belong to grows more fruitful and effectual, and, thus, we as individuals are made stronger as both givers and receivers in faith.

Reflection

1. What is your current experience of church? What can you remember about your earliest experiences of church? What similarities and differences have you experienced in church over time?

2. How have other members of the body of Christ helped you grow spiritually?

3. How can you encourage your church to be intercultural and intersectional so that all people can be welcomed and embraced?

YOUR KINGDOM COME

Your kingdom come. Your will be done,
on earth as it is in heaven.

—Matthew 6:10

If there is one thing I have learned from foreigners who visit America it is that we are living in remarkable and insidious abundance. Our food, entertainment, housing, appearance, behavior, and social ideology all reflect the abundance that seems to be tied to our cultural identity of freedom.

There is an idea that, in a meritocratic society, social mobility is granted to those who actively pursue it and that they will be able to live a dream life, an "American Dream" life, if they work hard enough to earn it. As a result, Americans are pressed on a desperate quest for something more. Everything in our pervasive media tells us that who we are and what we have is not enough: not successful enough, beautiful enough, new enough, big enough, or satisfying enough. We long for that higher paying job, that bigger home, that newer car, that farther vacation, or that bigger ring to convince ourselves that we are okay—or at the very least, better than the person next to us. Our ideas of fulfillment have been confused with materiality and attainment, rendering us insatiably greedy and spiritually impoverished.

We want stuff. We need stuff. It fills up the empty space around us, it fills up our time, and it fills up our minds. We work ourselves until the end just so we can reach another benchmark of "success" and find ourselves still lacking and still empty. What do we do when we are constantly made to feel as though we are behind in our lives and lacking something that proves our worth, our power, our influence, our very meaning? How are we meant to express our significance as a human being?

This question is where so many of us diverge into the dark and fall victim to the seductive powers of greed and egoism. In our loss of balance/perspective, we try to center our lives around the things that seem most gratifying, when in reality the only thing we need to center life around is our faith—our God. We read scripture and try to make sense of faith in our lives. We read scripture and try to simply make sense of living. This is what gives us inner peace and allows us to meditate on our individual power. We recite creeds and we even pray the Lord's Prayer. In that particular prayer, we come across the line "Your kingdom come."

When I was studying for my PhD, one of my professors asked our class what it meant when we express in the Lord's Prayer, "Your kingdom come." It was the first time I had ever questioned the meaning of the expression. I felt as though he had asked a trick question. Not only did I say the Lord's Prayer during the many times that I attended church in a week, but I also said the Lord's Prayer every morning at school. I recited the prayer at school, home, and church, and I even came to memorize it in two other languages, but I still had no idea what it was that I was saying.

It turned out no one else in class could provide the right answer either. He later answered his question, "When we pray in the Lord's Prayer, 'Your kingdom come,' it means, '(Let) *my* kingdom go.'"

Ultimately in saying this, I took in that during our journey to accepting God and reaching God's kin-dom, we must let go of the kingdoms or realms that we call our own and spend our lives trying to embellish. We build larger homes, garner more attention on social media, and accumulate more material goods as we try to ornament our little realms in light of our selfish and earthly desires.

We have to understand that God has a promised place, where in his son's saving incarnation—persecution, death, and resurrection—God has made a realm that is not yet consummated. With this in mind, we have to acknowledge that we are living in an in-between time, where we exist between the ascension of Jesus and his second coming. It tells us that Jesus' return will include God's judgment on us and the full consummation of God's realm.

So when we ask ourselves what more we need to feel fulfilled, the question answers itself. We do not need anything more. We are enough.

What we need to act upon, however, is different. We need to bring ourselves into the right way of thinking, one that diverges from materiality and dissatisfaction and towards hope for humanity's greater good derived from finding faith in God. The kin-dom of God, under the direction of Jesus, must come and save woman and man from themselves. Under God's kin-dom, human nature will be changed from its own self-detriment as we follow God's ultimate plans towards justness, peace, and morality.

That resonating idea from my professor years ago altered the way in which I see God and my material world, giving me insight into the temporality of status ambitions. It gave me the knowledge to give meaning to word, healing me to recognize how we are so caught up in the chase for more and that the only solution must be to let all our material desires go. This will set us free. This is a prayer that we need to pray daily, and this is the prayer we must be mindful of as we ultimately ask God to come and enter in.

Reflection

1. How much is enough? One closet, one home, one car? How are we consumed with building our own little kingdoms?

2. How can we live out the Lord's Prayer? While it isn't easy to do, what are some steps that we can take?

SEEING IS BELIEVING

They said to each other, "Were not our hearts burning
within us while he was talking to us on the road,
while he was opening the scriptures to us?"

—Luke 24:32

I grew up being an avid watcher of the television show, *Ripley's Believe It or Not!* In the 1980s, I sat right in front of the television in anticipation of the extraordinary men who pulled giant trucks using only their teeth, motorcyclists doing long-arching jumps over rows of wooden barrels, the fastest talkers and backward singers in the world, and even those bizarre humans who would eat airplanes and automotive vehicles piece by piece. That was the exact kind of entertainment I happily lost time to weekly. The show began in a mundane manner, introducing seemingly normal people doing normal things in their day-to-day lives and left you to watch in amazement at what they would do next. The premise of the show was that you really had to see it to believe it. The loyalty of their viewership came from dedication to visual and visceral wonder, keeping viewers hopeful for reliable entertainment. The seeing was the true wonder.

In the case of our personal faith, it is quite the opposite. We believe in an invisible God. We have faith in something we are never privy to. Yet somehow, we always find a way to see God in everything.

It is common to see faces in inanimate objects. This is called *pareidolia*, a psychological phenomenon that leads the brain to impart significance to facial features in random patterns. This may give reason as to why so many have believed they have seen Jesus in various objects. There are always stories of people saying that they have seen Jesus in some form or another, like on a piece of toast, on a potato chip, or on the grains of a wooden door. We are inclined to see a visual sign that God really exists, convincing ourselves that we need a radical symbol, a sign from above to have some verity in our faith. I believe that many have been eager to proclaim that they have seen Jesus in an inanimate object to give them a sense that, because they see God, they must be seen by God. But true faith is not led by mere perception and physical evidence. It is understood and felt.

If you try to see the world around you apart from the mere physical, you can understand that God does not physically inhabit creation any more than a painter inhabits her painting. Nevertheless, a painting can give us an understanding about the artist who painted it. God does not dwell in the material universe, but the observable universe reveals God's "invisible properties" that pervade everything that surrounds us and everything that sustains us in life: wisdom, hope, and love.

If we push ourselves to see the world in a similar light, we can recognize the presence of Jesus everywhere we turn: in the faces of strangers, in the poor, the hungry, and the imprisoned; we see him in our backyard, in the trees that surround us, in the earth that softens under our feet, and in the ocean that fills our world. We see him in the nature that gives us life all around, in those who have faith, and in those who suffer the most. If we understand that God is not simply observable in these things, but the life-giving omniscient spirit to these things, then we must reform the way in which we view them and treat them.

This view should make all the difference in how we take positive action. It gives us agency to push for justice. We must push for justice for the environment, living wages, health reform, and prison reform; we need to push for every action that fights for the causes in our world that need the most support. We need to protect these things in the same way we protect those we love: our family, our friends, and our Creator. We need to understand that belief is enough, and that those who have not seen but continue to believe are the blessed ones. So while you may not be exposed to, witness, or be affected by to the extreme poverty or the natural disasters caused by the ecological crisis, you serve to alleviate them because you believe them nonetheless—you serve God because you are strengthened in your faith.

The Christian faith is different from what the world teaches. The Christian faith is not "seeing is believing," but rather, "believing is seeing." We must open our eyes and hearts and see Jesus' presence in our lives. We need to see him in the places that we dare not to look and dare not to think about.

We serve an invisible God. No one has seen the shape of God, or heard God's voice, or felt God's physical embrace. But this does not stop us in our faith. This is what makes Christianity so wonderful. We understand that the most perfect, most certain, and most necessary things to our being, like love, like hope, are what cannot be seen, but felt.

Reflection

1. How have you seen Jesus in the stranger and in the poor?

2. How does seeing Jesus around us change how we live?

3. How does the presence of Jesus in our lives give us hope during our times of hardship?

LIVING IN GOD'S GRACE

Lent

But each of us was given grace according
to the measure of Christ's gift.

—*Ephesians 4:7*

Fact checking is simple in the information age. Regardless of who we are, exaggerations or embellishments are now easy to debunk with a quick internet search. However, for public figures, small investigations become amplified into an endless search for the truth, and the often defiant clarification of those in question leads to a domino-effect destruction of their public image. But often, the lines between misconstruing and misremembering become blurred, and intentions go from being innocuous to malicious. Through social media and the mainstream news, the significant, banal, untrustworthy, and divisive inundate us everywhere.

Most of the time, fact checking exposes an audience to a plethora of stories that would otherwise remain hidden or unknown. But in more recent times, it has lost its purpose and responsibility, algorithmically customized to suit one's internet history. It gives us the facade of diverse opinion and a breadth of news coverage, but in reality it offers a thinly skewed sketch of what is happening in the world based on click-bait titles hand-fed to us by artificial media curation. Our brief online skimmings of the world have given many of us the false idea that we are informed, knowledgeable, and worthy of distributing information that we ourselves are not sure is factual. This presupposition has also allowed us to "make or break" individuals without fully understanding the entire circumstances they were in.

On social media the salaciousness of the past floods us. "Breaking news" often gloats in the disparagement of public figures falling from the heights of their revered thrones. This is exactly what happened to renowned news anchor and journalist Brian Williams. During a New York Rangers hockey game, Brian Williams played tribute to a retired soldier by thanking him on camera for protecting him and his camera crew in Iraq in 2003 when the helicopter they were riding was forced down by enemy fire. The story was later revealed to be embellished, recounting that while he was indeed in a helicopter in Iraq with his camera crew in 2003, he was not fired on, rather it was another helicopter an hour ahead of him. When the story grew after his repeated retelling, journalists went through archival media to find out where he started to change his helicopter story. When the news broke, it was major scandal. In addition to the six months unpaid suspension, his career and public perception were tainted.

How can a much loved journalist and anchor of NBC's top-rated *Nightly News* program fall from such formidable heights? It isn't much of a surprise in a media-obsessed culture that enthralls itself with human error, creating a hungry audience that grows to anticipate the thrill of sensational falls from grace. This tendency can be attributed to the recent and increasingly frequent experiences of prominent news commentators and politicians who not only knowingly and systematically ignore the truth but propagate flagrant lies to gain political traction and distress their opposition. However, what we fail to acknowledge is the difference between facts and intention—or perhaps even the lack of intention—behind the person who may be sharing the facts.

We are all complicit in committing similar mistakes, exaggerating our own life experiences and stories for effect. We are also guilty of committing such mistakes unintentionally, as our memory fades and our wishes begin to color our past. This often happens with couples who have very different versions of how they first met.

Recounting and remembering past events differently at different moments in time happens to the best of us. When it does, we hope that no one will catch us, or at least that they will smile through it knowingly amidst an evening conversation. But must we always be on guard? Must we live in fear of accidentally relaying false experiences or exaggerating? Is it malicious if we fail to think it through? More importantly, do we really want to live in an environment where we actively anticipate untruthfulness from others and strip them of their dignity?

In Christian faith, we often talk about grace. Augustine explains that the Holy Spirit gives us grace. Grace is a gift from God: a gift we did not deserve, but a gift freely given to us. As we experience and reflect on the phenomena of monitoring and pouncing on other's mistakes, it is also wise for us to reread the Sermon on the Mount. In Matthew 5:22, for example, we are instructed to forgive our brothers and sisters before we expect to get any satisfaction from the Lord. God's word to us is to get our own house in order before beseeching him for any kind of forgiveness. Remember that line in the Lord's Prayer, "forgive us our trespasses as we forgive those who trespass against us." Grace is about giving others second chances.

Where would we be—where would life be—without the offering of a second chance? As a parent, what would happen to our children if we never extended second chances to them?

In the church, where we are supposed to experience grace and extend grace to one another, we often do the opposite. In experiencing critical treatment from others, we feel like it is acceptable to return the same judgment and harsh criticism as "punishment." We long to accept grace for our own lives and struggle to offer it into other people's lives. But to receive grace is to live through grace.

Every year, we begin Lent on Ash Wednesday. Lent is the period of prayer, penance, repentance, and atonement before Easter Sunday during which we prepare our hearts to understand the meaning of the cross. It is a time to reflect on our own lives and the life of Jesus and what Jesus has done for us. If Jesus understands our own evil and sinful nature and, in spite of it, extends grace to us, then shouldn't we match his actions as well? We see the ultimate second chance through Jesus' death. God shows love and mercy to us over and over again, giving us the second chance at life through the death of his only son. Forgiving others is tied to our own forgiveness; thus we should find delight in showing mercy unto others. Life should provide the opportunity to both give and receive second chances.

As we pray and repent during this season of Lent, we should practice, embody, and extend grace. If we see a co-worker, friend, or family member make a mistake, rather than turn away in judgment and position ourselves on higher ground than them, we should extend our hearts, show our compassion as fallible beings, and lend our hand to live out grace. Even Brian Williams received grace and is back on TV as a news anchor. By walking alongside those who are in need of a second chance, we bring greater healing into their lives and, thus, shine light onto God's kin-dom.

Reflection

1. Where have you experienced God's grace in your life?

2. How have you shared God's grace with those in need? How do we extend God's grace to others?

3. The Bible speaks about being "saved by God's grace." What does this mean for you in your life?

JESUS AND THE CROSS
Good Friday

As they entered the tomb, they saw a young man, dressed in a white robe, sitting on the right side; and they were alarmed. But he said to them, "Do not be alarmed; you are looking for Jesus of Nazareth, who was crucified. He has been raised; he is not here. Look, there is the place they laid him. But go, tell his disciples and Peter that he is going ahead of you to Galilee; there you will see him, just as he told you."

—Mark 16:5–7

He was despised and rejected by others; a man of suffering, and acquainted with infirmity; and as one from whom others hide their faces he was despised, and we held him of no account.

—Isaiah 53:3

Rejection is a recurring part of life. It is an unavoidable part of being human, and despite the fact that we all experience it, being rejected isolates us in our experience, making us feel as though we are the only ones who have been cast aside and left unwanted. Personally, I am still fearful of it. Yet, we experience rejection and its pain from an early age and continue to feel its blows throughout every stage of life. Whether you were socially outcast, rejected from a job, turned down by a love interest, or left out from a classmate's birthday party, the feeling of refusal is never one that you welcome.

It's the classic rejection scenario. As an unathletic kid in elementary school, I would anxiously wait to be picked by team leaders during gym class and school field days. Remaining by the sidelines, I slowly watched my surrounding classmates get selected one by one until I was the last one standing. I steadily felt myself dissipating into nothing, and when I finally got called last, I vanished into thin air.

I know this to be a universal experience as a child. We all go through rough patches of social rejections as we come into our own and try to understand where we fit in relation to our environment. My more poignant rejection came later, during my junior prom. I exhausted myself debating whether or not I should ask a boy I had a crush on. He was everything that a teenage girl could have wanted, a handsome senior at another high school who also happened to be a musician. I swear, I dreamt about it in my sleep, sifting through every possible scenario in my head; I went on to discuss it for days with all my friends, going over and over it with them until the deliberation ran its course. Of course, being the supportive friends they were, they eventually encouraged me to ask him out, even assuring me that there would be no way he would say no. So over the next few days, I worked up the courage and recited my words. I got his number from a friend, and finally bit the bullet and called. It was going to be effortless, painless, rewarding—but as soon as he picked up the phone, I choked. He sounded tired and a bit confused as to why I was calling him. I was silent for a bit until I nervously pushed out some contrived small-talk and stumbled my way on to asking him the question: "Do you want to go to prom with me?" He responded after a long silence, "um, well...I—I'm actually trying to work things out with my ex...sorry." I felt myself again disappear into nothing. Mortified, but still attempting to keep my cool, I replied a bit too quickly, "Just crossed my mind, don't worry about it." I hung up the phone, cried, and repeated the conversation in my head in complete shame. For weeks I was down about it; I didn't want to face my friends, and I certainly was done ever speaking to the boy. I think back on it now and laugh about it, but at the time I truly believed that there was no getting over it.

The way we react to rejection is based on the elements and the events of our past. And as a result, the way in which we respond to rejection is typically equally or more significant than the rejection itself. This is why it is so important for us to shift our perspective around rejection, seeking self-understanding and acceptance in order to feel more confident in coping with the present struggle while confronting the future.

We experience frivolous rejections, devastating rejections, and course-changing rejections, but Jesus knew the damnation of rejection most eminently. The people of Nazareth, his own hometown, rejected him (Luke 4:26–30). Still others wondered about him because of that hometown. "Nathanael said to him, 'Can anything good come out of Nazareth?'" (John 1:46). People rejected much of his teaching. Many questioned the origin of his teachings and did not accept him because he was born poor, the son of Joseph the carpenter. In Matthew 21:42, Jesus talks about the stone the builders rejected. The story is a revelation about Jesus himself.

The Gospels say that Jesus traveled a lot and suggest he entered villages where he found no place to rest. Luke's Gospel tells of a time when Jesus was not welcomed in a Samaritan village (Luke 9:51–53). Jesus' comment on the experience could imply this happened frequently (Luke 9:58).

Remember the last few hours of Jesus' life before his crucifixion. There were many people and groups who rejected Jesus at his end, including those closest to him. Judas betrayed Jesus and identified him in the Garden of Gethsemane for those who came to arrest him. The disciples all ran away in fear when Jesus was arrested. Peter, who said that he would never desert Jesus, ended up denying Jesus three times (John 18:15–27). The high priest, chief priests, elders, and scribes rejected Jesus and sought to put him to the most excruciating, demoralizing death.

The religious leaders took Jesus to Pilate for a trial. Pilate did not want any trouble, and since it was the governor's custom to release one prisoner during Passover, he asked the crowd, "Whom do you want me to release for you, Jesus Barabbas or Jesus who is called the Messiah?" (Matthew 27:17). The crowds chose Barabbas and rejected Jesus, leaving him to be crucified.

At the final moment of his life, Jesus felt the ultimate rejection. On the cross at the ninth hour Jesus cries out "My God, my God, why have you forsaken me?" (Matthew 27:45). Jesus knows and understands rejection; in fact, he exemplified it.

Tremendous pain comes with rejection. The experience can feel like one has been thrown into a spiraling end, an emotional and spiritual black hole leading us to wonder why it is we who have to suffer, why it is we who have to unrightfully endure such pain. But like all suffering, rejection punctuates life. Rejection is necessary to our human experience, to life itself. We may experience rejection from a lover or a family member. We may experience rejection from a community or society at large; whether it stems from our appearance, preferences, background, or any other aspect of our personhood, all forms of rejection cause pain and add temporary obstructions on our life paths. Yet, as we remember Jesus, we know that his experience of rejection and crucifixion on that wooden cross did not end the story, because rejection is another beginning. Rejection turns our chin toward a direction we were not once privy to and are not yet accepting of. Rejection is an introduction to the new.

God had the final word: a word of life and love. Holy Week in our church calendar had a wondrous and miraculous outcome. In the pain and experience of rejection, there is hope. In our misery and suffering, there is resurrection and new life.

As the sun seems to set during our moments of rejection, darkness, and desolation, we can live with the hope that the sun will rise. We find connection in our suffering, self-love over our self-judgment, and new discoveries arising from pathways that were placed for us to find while we search in pain. Despite the inevitability of rejection, we are reminded that God greets us all with open arms for embrace and for the ultimate welcoming of love in our lives.

Reflection

1. Share some of your experiences of rejection. Were all these experiences painful?

2. How do you survive rejection? What are some of your strategies?

3. How do you participate in rejecting others? We are to welcome all people regardless of skin, sexuality, gender, etc. Do we do this? Or is it easier for us to resort to rejection?

4. Jesus welcomes all of us. How do we enact this in our communities?

REIMAGINING

Easter

For in Christ Jesus you are all children of God through faith.
As many of you as were baptized into Christ have clothed
yourselves with Christ. There is no longer Jew or Greek, there
is no longer slave or free, there is no longer male and female;
for all of you are one in Christ Jesus. And if you belong to
Christ, then you are Abraham's offspring, heirs according to
the promise.

—Galatians 3:26–29

Women have always been actively involved in the church. We see
evidence of this in the Bible. One of the most famous instances is
Mary, the first evangelist, running out of Jesus' tomb, excited to
share the news of Jesus' resurrection with others. It was Mary who
ran and told Peter and John about the radical good news that she
had just witnessed.

When Paul writes his letters to Corinthians telling women to
be silent, it is an indication that women were actually present in the
church, speaking, teaching, and leading. If they were not, Paul
would not have made the effort to silence these women. As a mother

of three, I try my best to never silence my children. I encourage their messy, loud honesty rather than the "dignified" suppression that I was enforced to follow in a conservative Korean household. Paul's attempt to restrain female involvement reveals that women were active in the early church and must have been speaking and teaching despite the cultural norms. To maintain the peace of supposed tradition in the church, Paul believed that the activity of women in the church had to be downplayed, stifled, and reduced. Despite the knowledge that women have been historically significant as a part of the church, the degree to which they have been ignored is alarming. In part, this has to do with the church's doctrine surrounding women.

Today, church teachings that continue to subordinate women in any capacity, explicitly or implicitly, should be heavily questioned—whether these teachings are told through the creation story, the Trinity, the sacraments, the meaning of crucifixion and resurrection, and more. Church doctrines form our thoughts and practices in the church; they inform how we view God, ourselves, each other, and the greater world. Because church doctrine is so powerful, all teachings that result in the oppression of half the world's population must to be critiqued, heavily reexamined, and effectively reimagined. Only when we begin this task of dismantling and rebuilding can the founding theology that has allowed the inequitable allotment of socio - economic power based on gender be liberated.

We also need to open ourselves up to new voices and opinions that divulge fragments of the pain and injustice that still exists in our churches.

We hope our individual voices will provide solidarity with women around the globe and continue to shift our theological understanding to one that uplifts oppressed groups and does not simply relegate women as "victims" or men as "assailants" in society. Women and men alike should not be differentiated for their presumed power, but held to equal standards of morality and behavior. To attain this balance, we must continue to offer and practice new ways of being and new ways of imagining; we hope these new voices will bring hope, peace, and justice to a world still functioning on antiquated systems that belie its modernity.

These new ways of imagining recognize that there are ideas that obscure reality and hide ecclesiastical imbalances. Reimagining requires courage as it summons us to leave our comfortable traditions and, in some cases, overturn them. The notion of reimagining comes with romantic illusions, as if it is a pursuit distanced from reality where visionary idealizations come to life. But in real use, the act of reimagining takes actual time and effort to initiate our first steps toward changing our faith and our churches. Reimagining also necessitates the action of risk-taking: a risk to make a mistake, a risk to lose what one has, a risk to feel betrayed by one's own people and to feel that you may be betraying them. It means being open to changing one's course and creating new ideas to both reform and enrich the old ones.

To take this risk, the church must re-examine what we know to be tradition and what we practice habitually in order to see the world from a modern, fully dimensional perspective. We need to stand in solidarity with women around the globe. Transcending our divergent backgrounds and personal stories is a common battle, one that can be strengthened by a global female union with a mission to see the reimagined come into existence. As women share more of their stories, the church must lie quiet and listen. It is a new process that will take time to grow out of its deep-rooted history but will be the essential reinvigoration that the church requires to thrive in the future. It lifts us up as we recognize the pain of our own stories in each other's. Through this sharing/reimagining, we become more whole, bursting with energy and spirit. Out of the pain of leaving familiar ideas behind, we recognize our solidarity with each other around the globe in theological and Christian innovation. Together we can utilize a progressive church doctrine that is fair, welcoming, and embracing of all people, uncategorized by gender, class, race, or geography.

Reflection

1. Do you experience gender injustice in your own life? Or in the church?

2. How does scripture view the role of women?

3. How can we work towards equality between men and women? How can we all participate to build gender equality?

SPIRIT FILLED

Pentecost

Then afterward I will pour out my spirit on all flesh;
your sons and your daughters shall prophesy, your old men
shall dream dreams, and your young men shall see visions.

—Joel 2:28

Growing up in the Presbyterian Church meant that there was not
much talk of the Holy Spirit. In most mainline denominations Jesus
is the primary focus of discussion; in my adolescent experience this
was also the case. Mentions of the Holy Spirit were sparse and
laden with vague ambiguity. The Spirit was not something I thought
about, nor was it something I thought actually existed. To me it was
just a word, an abstract concept that materialized in the Bible for
effect. However, when my father dragged our family across the
U.S.-Canadian border in times he felt immured by his job, city,
home, and frustrating financial circumstances, we found ourselves
in Detroit for a change of scenery. There were a few years in the
mid 1970s where he would pack my mom, my sister, and me into
the car like sardines and make the trip to the United States. At first
it was exciting, but in time, I grew to be extremely uneasy of what

was to come. Because there, in the fringes of downtown Detroit, we would attend Pentecostal revival services.

It was during these Pentecostal revival services that I first encountered the Spirit. I remember one intense, confusing, untamed weekend where, during one of the children's Bible study classes, I heard strange noises emerging from a large backroom. Curious, I wandered out and followed the sounds towards a door left ajar, momentarily glimpsing a revival service. What I saw in the backroom was indecipherable. There, as a piano played, I witnessed adults speak in tongues, pray fanatically, fall to the ground as their knees gave in, cry and scream in panic, and dance in the Spirit. As a young girl I was petrified, not just because it was such a jarring sight, but because they seemed to have no control over what was happening to themselves. Adults, who minutes before had been smiling and politely greeting one another, had been seemingly taken over by another entity. I had little idea what had taken them over, but all I knew was that they were supposedly encountering, feeling, and living through the Spirit, and thus I was by affect as well.

The early revival service encounter was significant to my understanding of the Spirit. It allowed me to question how the Spirit could elicit such a response from those it touched. I have now come to understand that during Pentecost the Spirit came down to fill and fulfill. It filled the people in that space then, just as it does me now. I now experience the Spirit as a powerful calm in moments of peace. It has come in times when I felt I could no longer go on and nudged me, moved me, and worked through me as an electrifying force. It has given me courage, and it has given me hope.

Integral to my work is to explore who God is, beyond and apart from the image constructed by Eurocentric Christianity. I participate in an abundance of multifaith dialogues, conferences, and meetings, a privilege that has allowed me to discover God through the eyes of the other. While scriptures and practices differ, every conversation I have had with those who engage in a differing faith has allowed me to unearth the reality that the Spirit is just as integral for them as it is for me.

The Spirit is integral to the full breadth of cultures and religions. This is evidenced by what many Africans have historically stated, saying that they had the Spirit long before white missionaries came onto their land. In Asian culture, Spirit has been part of the religion and culture for thousands of years. Though a religion or culture may use a different word for spirit, such as geist, Chi, pana, and more, the meaning and understanding is transcendent and universal.

If disparate cultures and religions all discuss the Spirit, then can it be the Spirit who brings the connected world of people together in peace? I believe so. We understand this through scripture, which recounts God pouring God's Spirit upon all people (Joel 2:28). It isn't just upon Egyptians or Israelites or modern Christians, but upon all people.

Through this universal understanding, we can elevate this unifying force, this Spirit, from the echelons of obscurity. We can understand its complexity through its simple action, which is that the Spirit of God gives us life, sustains us, and brings us joy, peace, and hope.

Reflection

1. What are your earliest experiences of encounters with the Spirit?

2. How do you feel the presence of the Spirit in your life?

3. How can we be aware of the presence of the Spirit in our faith as well as in other religious traditions around the world?

LIVING IN CULTURE

We all belong to a culture. It is what makes us, us. Culture is the collective human behavior, ideas, and customs of a group of people. Everything we know to be a part of our way of life resides in this collective manifestation: family is culture; wearing clothes is culture; going to church is culture; waving "hello" is culture. Culture is a part of our learned behavior and provides an omnipresent framework for the way in which we choose to act, think, and participate in our society. America has a culture of individualism, capitalism, economic mobility, and social freedom. This has allowed for great liberties in creating the much pursued "American Dream," where any individual is granted the opportunity to construct the "dream life" for themselves. But for many of us, the dream life seems to be a distant fantasy.

The culture that we are immersed in today has never been more saturated with information. So infinite is this information in its innovation and growing access that its permeation will only become more pervasive and integral to the human experience. This infinite exposure has made many of us feel as though we are lagging or inconsequential, overwhelming us with the anxiety that the lives we are living are insignificant. Undoubtedly, this feeling has always captured us in the past, but with unfettered globalization and digital connection we must ask ourselves how to cope with such a tool.

Perhaps we can begin to do so through changing our approach. Maybe what we need is to garner meaningful, positive intention in the boundless platforms of unregulated content and interaction. Through any channel or medium, the information and visual culture we consume should be viewed with a critical eye. It should be consumed with constant self-reflection.

As we are more vulnerable, gullible, and partial than many likely believe, in opening our minds to the rapid pace of change we must also refuse blind embrace. Accepting this vulnerability will give us the faculty of objectivity that allows us to observe and listen more consciously.

In the digital age, we should not only consider the issues that are brought forth with technology but the extreme privilege that it has brought us. Today, we are more fortunate a society than in any other era. Poverty, disease, world hunger, and religious, racial, and sexual conflict are statistically lower than any other time in history. The global living standard is at an all-time high, leading us to live longer, healthier lives. With this state of burgeoning progress, we all have an opportunity to contribute to this enduring change because, intentionally or not, we all participate in revolutionizing culture through reimagination. But now, try and use your intentions for imagining what kind of world you would like to live in. Envision a realistic version of this imaginary world. How do people interact? How do we live with one another? Is this the kind of world you want your children or grandchildren to live in? Is this the kind of world that you want for future generations to thrive in? If we envision a world we hope for, then we can answer the final question positively and, likely, quite simply. We can all easily envision a rosier version of our world, but we must take reimagination a step further and put it into action. We must remind ourselves of the responsibilities we have in the present, to reshape a future that is more ethically inclined. Through positively reforming our thoughts, we can influence behavior; in changing individual behavior, we can influence communal action; in changing communal action, we can change our collective culture.

This section focuses on committing to this endeavor: to examine and reimagine our current culture. Through subjects as familiar as loving our neighbors, to the grandiosity of gender justice, to the contemporary influence of celebrity and beauty, we will set foot into the pervasive, to confront our reticent inner selves.

THE RACIALIZATION OF BEAUTY

> Do not adorn yourselves outwardly by braiding your hair, and
> by wearing gold ornaments or fine clothing; rather, let your
> adornment be the inner self with the lasting beauty of a
> gentle and quiet spirit, which is very precious in God's sight.
>
> —*1 Peter 3:3–4*

I grew up worshiping fashion magazines. Without much other avail-
able abundant material, out of date, crinkled, read-over fashion
publications my parents picked up for free became the first written
material to truly influence me in my early adolescence. While I did
not realize it then, it was affirming a disturbing reality: there was
something the world knew as beautiful and I was not it.

I can recall one of my first times going through a summer edi-
tion of an American fashion magazine, becoming wholly entranced
at the otherworldly glamour of beautiful white women sprawled
across double-page spreads; they smoldered right past me, looking
as though they were aware of their bewitched, awed viewer. I developed a paradoxical infatuation with these fair-skinned, big-eyed,
long-legged beauties, loving them and hating them and obsessing
over them, thinking to myself, "if only I…" Like many young girls,
these images tuned my barometer of physical beauty. I studied them,

comparing them against one another and then myself. I dreamed about the day when I would miraculously wake up as beautiful, discovering my big blue eyes and long blond hair. This dream only exacerbated as I grew into my teens and I descended into an incomprehensible depressive state to indulge my self-loathing. I looked around and didn't see a reflection of myself, and I started to understand that my physical value was merely tangential to my community and in the culture.

Flipping through these magazines, which had not the slightest representation of Asian Americans, left a profound imprint on me. It informed me as to what beauty looked like, what people wanted to see as a result, and what existed as the unquestionable representational norm of life. It has imparted a manipulated self-image and paved the way for what I now know as the westernization of beauty.

Today, as a middle-aged woman, I rarely read magazines anymore, but when I do, I am both aggravated and bored by how beauty has remained largely stagnant in its representation. Of course, the fashion, beauty, and advertising landscape has revolutionized and craned towards the safe politically correct agenda, but the change feels as though they are merely representing "unconventional" bodies as a moralistic token. The "standards of beauty" have mirrored globalized and modern revelations. The advertisements, runway shots, cover girls, and photo stories all try to convey the standards of beauty that their audience is urged to follow and aspire towards. The standards are still largely influenced by the Eurocentric history of luxury fashion, and the contemporary North American version aligns with such antiquated paradigms. The beauty ideal is fueled by the unattainable majority of "aspirational" advertising, which is biased toward the fairness of skin and sample-sized bodies. Advertisements support the Euro-American male appetite for feminine beauty, created in Paris, Milan, London, and New York City.

In more recent times, the appropriation of Black features and culture has been absorbed into the mainstream. Many of us non-Black public figures are able to see the exploitation and appropriation of Black physicality, culture, diction, and lexicon. Characteristics such as full lips, Black hair styles, and augmented bottoms, hips, and breasts are all qualities that African American women have been judged harshly upon in the past and are now exploited and reproduced by dominant white society for its new trendy, sexualized appeal.

When you think about the first time you ever viewed someone as beautiful, who comes to mind? Was this individual someone who fit into this standard? Were they a part of the standard? Did they look like you? While the issue is complicated, we largely tend to judge our own beauty according to the people we find attractive. When I think of the first time I ever thought of someone as beautiful, it was my second-grade school teacher. She was a white woman with long, sleek black hair, dark brown eyes, and translucent pale skin. I thought she was the most beautiful woman I had ever seen. And in some ways, I was partial to her look because I could see something of myself in her darker features. As an Asian American woman without "white skin," light hair, and large round eyes, there was no one—even in my own Asian community—who told me I was attractive.

I grew up with young Korean girls who deeply internalized that being beautiful meant to look white. Asians today still revere whiteness as the pinnacle of beauty. I had many girlfriends who wished they had bigger eyes, so they would carve out slivers of scotch tape and adhere it to their eyelids to attain the infamous "double eyelid," the fold on the lid of an eye that creates a folded crease and adds depth to the eye socket.

This is the same story that Julie Chen shared as a co-host of the television program *The Talk*. Her boss told her that her eyes "look disinterested" and she could never become an anchor on the news channel with her appearance. To even get a chance at being on TV, she underwent double-eyelid surgery, a common cosmetic procedure done by East-Asian women. It is not an isolated story, but an extremely common one of Asian women who internalize the notion that their natural, classic Asian features will withhold them from success in their careers and relationships. We have changed our faces to subtly assimilate into a more Western appearance. This plays out in various cultures through numerous changes in idealization of beauty in Asia. Be it in China, India, Malaysia, or Korea, white skin, large eyes, a high nose bridge and a smaller face is the ultimate indication of beauty—features that conflict with more typical Asian features of wider facial structures, flatter noses, narrow eyes, and diverse skin tones. While some Asians will purport that these Asian beauty standards are not in acquiescence to white beauty, the correlated disposition to these characteristics does not seem to be a mere coincidence.

Added to these artificial standards of beauty are magazines like *People* who choose "the most beautiful person of the year." The standards of beauty used to make the selection are arbitrary, personal, and based on an established system governed by conventional Western standards. How can any magazine judge the beauty of individuals and determine who the most beautiful person in the world is, when it sees beauty through an exclusively white lens? Is there a way to rank or measure beauty that is unbiased? Are we meant to uphold such merit to those who are seen as beautiful? I detest it when *People* magazine chooses the "most beautiful woman of the year." This pushes a cycle perpetuated by the idea that women have to compete against one another based on their appearance, extending the notion that women have to sustain and fit into a physical criterion to achieve any kind of success, which men have a lesser obligation towards. I am not interested in seeing how the magazine validates its own whiteness as a standard of beauty and aspiration.

However, in 2014 *People* magazine made the decision to nominate Lupita Nyong'o as the most beautiful person of the year. Nyong'o is a Mexican-born Kenyan actress who is dark skinned. She has been transparent in her own struggle with the darkness of her skin, especially in the context of Black beauty. Colorism is still a highly divisive tool with a powerful history in America. It allows for the assignment of beauty through perceived power, where dark-skinned Blacks are less visible, less celebrated, and less represented than light-skinned Blacks in our culture and media. This is also the result of the white-led media consistently reinforcing the idea that even though people of color are now seen, their beauty is still regulated and monitored under Western convention. However, Nyong'o's win should keep us pushing for more: we need to ask ourselves, when will more unconventional versions of minority women be on the fronts of magazines in their fullness of being (not conventionally thin, air-brushed, or lightened on covers)? We must make sure the media industry doesn't pat itself on the back for token representations and forget about real change. We need to keep asking for more. We need to challenge and redefine the conventional standards of beauty to include women and men of all colors, shapes, abilities, backgrounds, and appearances. Once dominant society and media truly accept and desire women from all ethnic backgrounds as beautiful, then we can begin to have young girls accept, welcome, and embrace their own dynamic inner beauty.

Reflection

1. Who can be the judge of beauty?

2. How can we dismantle Western racialization of beauty?

3. What are the steps to embrace one's inner beauty?

4. If we are all created by God, are we not all beautiful? How do we embrace our inner and outer beauty, which God has given to us?

THE ASIAN AMERICAN "BUTTERFLY"

Love does no wrong to a neighbor;
therefore, love is the fulfilling of the law.

—Romans 13:10

Asian Americans have been in the United States since the 1800s, but the Asian American experience has been perpetually left out of the historical narrative. Our presence is often overlooked within discourses on race, ethnicity, racism, and prejudice, reflecting a long-spanning sentiment that we are not significant to the country's cultural fabric. The long history of Asians as indentured workers, miners, and railroad workers has shaped the growth, expansion, and stability of America, which has been persistently dismissed through our omission in America's history.

To remember the contributions of Asian Americans to the United States, Congress designated the first ten days of May as Asian-Pacific Heritage Week in 1977: a time to remember the long legacy of historic, economic, and social contributions made to the building of America by Asian Americans and Pacific Islanders. Observances continued, in 1992 when Congress passed a law designating May as Asian American and Pacific Islander Heritage Month.

While it is exciting to reflect on these national observances during this month, it is also imperative that we address the deep-seated racism that is still in affect against many Asian American Pacific Islanders (AAPI), especially women from those cultures. We may be familiar with the story of Giacomo Puccini's *Madama Butterfly*, an operatic narrative that reflects on the reality for many people of color in America. The underlying story is true, based on an autobiographical novel, *Madame Chrysanthème* by Pierre Loti. The story of *Madama Butterfly* begins with a U.S. Navy officer named Pinkerton, who wishes to marry a fifteen-year-old Japanese girl, Cio-Cio San (Butterfly), for convenience until he finds an American wife. This story revealed an internal perspective of how AAPI women had been viewed and treated by dominant white society and the ways in which the archetypal perception of Asians and Asian American relationships continues to prevail today.

Shortly after he leaves for the United States, Pinkerton gets married. Butterfly faithfully waits for him and gives birth to their son without him. After three years living partnerless, Butterfly receives news that Pinkerton is coming back to see her. Her heart swoons, but little does she know he has married a white American woman during the time of his absence.

Butterfly was used as a temporary wife in an expedient marriage without her knowledge. Additionally, through this polarizing foreign marriage, she becomes alienated from her own family. To finalize Butterfly's tragedy, Pinkerton and his new spouse decide to come back because the American wife has agreed to raise the Japanese American child. Once Butterfly realizes the true intention of Pinkerton's visit, to take their child back with him, she agrees to the request in obedient acquiescence. She then blindfolds the child for sendoff and commits suicide.

This is the agonizing finale to what Butterfly thought was her love story, when in truth she was only used as a sexual partner while the naval officer was lonely and far from home. To Pinkerton, Butterfly was a commodity, not a person in her own right. He gave his young bride the name "Butterfly" because he did not even know her Japanese name and wanted to regard her by a title of his own volition. By relegating her to the fleeting, vainly beautiful world of nature, she became a creature of background, a mere peripheral allure in the centrality of the white American man. To use German Lutheran theologian Rudolf Otto's terminology, Pinkerton viewed Butterfly as an "it" rather than a "thou."

We are all too familiar with this narrative. It is the story of a white man marrying a foreign Asian woman out of convenience for his pleasure. The white man can think of her as a utile accessory, using his position of power to attain her and maintain her, then discarding her at a beneficial time and preventing her from mingling American and Asian cultures.

Today, AAPIs encounter racism, prejudice, and stereotyping in all aspects of life through explicit or, now more commonly, micro-aggressed means. The latter is the more common form of racism that prevails today, also often occurring in our churches and faith communities under innocuous veils of religion. Even the perpetrator may not realize their own complicity or contribution to it, just as their counterpart may not realize it as well. For Asians this is the kind of polite, educated, seemingly well-intentioned indirect racism we have had to face for most of recent history. We have accepted it and internalized it to the point that we often express racism towards ourselves as an act of power repossession and social safety.

In the United States, AAPI women are still often viewed as foreigners who are hyper-sexualized and thought of as passive subordinates by male counterparts. Asian American men, on the other hand, have been stripped of their sexuality, being demasculinized, feminized, and dismissed as potential partners or individuals in positions of power. The effect of this stereotype on men has been so powerful that even modern Asian American women undermine and dismiss them in agreement to the stereotypical perceptions.

We are viewed as "perpetual foreigners" in the background of popular culture and simply white noise in the landscape of social and political action. It does not matter how many generations one has been in the United States, AAPIs look different and have strong aesthetic associations to the stereotypes associated with the Korean and Vietnamese war from the 1950s and '70s. AAPIs have been living in the United States for many generations, yet continue to be exoticized because of our physical distinction. In response, we alter the size and color of our eyes, the shape of our nose, and the color of our skin to construct a distinct mutation towards Westernized features. The notion that many consider AAPIs to be the "model minority" or "honorary whites" is no relief. It is another version of prejudice that is camouflaged in artificial positivism and kidnaps our true value as diverse individuals in the collective tapestry of minorities in America.

As a result, AAPI women continue to be mistreated, objectified, trivialized, and subordinated by the media and dominant society. The trope we see in *Madama Butterfly* is personally close to me. I know "Butterflies" in my own life. I grew up with them; they are my family, my friends, and familiar strangers—they are me. Nevertheless, like all marginalized groups, we must recognize that we are all created in God's image. Therefore, we need to actively confront and challenge any form of racism or sexism that permeates our society and faith communities.

Celebrate the rich AAPI history during the month of May and remember the story of *Madama Butterfly*. Keep in mind how racism and sexism breed subtly and indirectly in our society. We have to become attuned to our own unconscious abetment that contributes to this culture. Seek to redefine, liberate, and pave the way for interracial justice, shalom, and equality.

Reflection

1. How does the Asian American community contribute to the wider society today?

2. Are you familiar with Asian American churches and faith communities? How can people of different ethnicities all worship and come together to be with God?

REMOVING THE SHAME
OF SEXUAL ASSAULT

So if anyone is in Christ, there is a new creation: everything
old has passed away; see, everything has become new!

—*2 Corinthians 5:17*

Recently with my daughter I watched the movie, *To All the Boys I
Loved Before,* a warm teen romantic comedy about a young girl confronting, well, all the boys she loved before. I was astonished with
the reveal of the romantic lead, an Asian American girl, and I was
surprised again with just how emotional I was to see her—to see a
face like hers, like mine, like my daughter's, like my mother's, as a
conduit for important cultural shifts. While it may seem like it to
many, minority representation has not come out of nowhere. It has
not happened as a spontaneous and righteous reaction to the white
supremacy of our media; rather, it has been slow, painful, and tumultuous road that has taken decades of pioneers, mavericks, and
change-makers to nudge our culture a few, albeit large, succession
of steps forward.

Watching Lana Condor, the lead in the teen film, made me think
of my own teen years and my own childhood. I thought of Connie
Chung, who resided as the fifth guest in my childhood home during

many nights of evening news. Chung was a significant figure in my social and cultural upbringing. It was my mother who actually insisted in keeping the news on, not because she had any particular interest in current news or even because she could fully understand what Chung was saying in English, but because she was simply thrilled to see Chung on screen. My mother thought Connie was one of the most beautiful women she had ever seen, and, because she was the only Asian woman anchor on television in the 1980s, my mother felt it was my conferred duty to support her through watching.

I grew to greatly admire Connie Chung. As an Asian American girl growing up in the 1980s, I had few Asian American woman role models to follow. Chung became my unspoken role model. I never talked to anyone about her, never gushed about her as many young teens would about their own role models, but she remained a powerful part of my media upbringing even as I matured and stopped watching NBC's evening news. It both reminded me and proved to me that women who looked like her could become someone with linguistic sovereignty and integral cultural capital. She spoke her mind and often shared her experience of being a radically challenging presence in a white male industry tied to the white patriarchal realms of mainstream media, politics, and journalism. This is especially relevant in the intersection of race and gender, as Asian women were and still are perceived to be submissive to the dominant.

That is why it was ever more remarkable that Chung, a Chinese American, revealed to the public her experience of sexual assault. In her open letter to another sexual assault victim, "Dear Christine Blasey Ford: I, too, was sexually assaulted—and it's seared into my memory forever,"[1] Connie reveals an experience that she carried for more than fifty years. She described it as her "dirty little secret,"

1. Connie Chung, "Dear Christine Blasey Ford: I, too, was sexually assaulted—and it's seared into my memory forever," *The Washington Post*, Oct 3, 2018.

something that was deeply buried in the past. In part, she reveals that it was due to her sexual naiveté at the time, but it was also for the hopeful protection of her own family. This illuminates an important effect of sexual assault where the incident brings shame upon the victim rather than the perpetrator. This is exacerbated if you come from a conservative culture, as most Asian Americans do, where "saving face" and bringing shame to the family or community—the collective group—is enough cause to stay silent. Statistics for sexual assault in Asian American communities are hard to come by, as there are limited ways in which we can study a group that has been wary of being vocal. However, a study by Asian Pacific Institute on Gender Based Violence found that anywhere from 21 to 55 percent of Asian American women report facing physical and or sexual violence in their lifetime. If we continue to support a culture of shame around survivors, it will persist, and Asian Americans will continue to fall silent in the pursuit of maintaining the peace in their communities and in their lives.

For Asian Americans this collective community is powerful; it is what nurtures us, cultivates us, protects us—and also what endangers us. This established system of sociocultural behavior creates bounding expectations that work to keep victims silent in fear of disgracing others and themselves. It is yet another complicated cultural layer of internalized degradation and self-persecution that women endure as sexual assault victims.

Connie Chung offered a window to the emotional experience and thought processes of sexual assault victims. While it may seem minor to some, it was extremely significant for me to see a woman of color, an Asian American woman, come forward to speak about this experience. This is why the capacities of representation are so wide and meaningful, as we use faces, bodies, and cultures akin to our own to find a semblance of ourselves—a reflection of our own significance.

Connie Chung's confession brought decades of my own suppression to a head. She did what she could to cope with the incident, which was to nullify all of the memories and emotional ramifications of the event. I did the same.

I was sexually assaulted by someone close to my family when I was a child. It was a painful, deeply suppressed burden that I carried in secret for my whole life up until now. I was incapable of understanding what had happened for years, and so afraid that I would shame my family, that I distanced myself from it. I distanced myself from it so far, for so long, that even now I think about it as a nightmare. I think about it as a horrifying dream, something that happened to me, but didn't really happen to *me*.

I'm now in my fifties and I still have difficulty thinking about that incident and trying to understand it. In the post-era of #MeToo, I hope people remember this movement as one that is not merely a social media trend or cultural fashion, but a long-awaited jolt against the abiding powers that have presided over our lives: something that is so innately imbedded in nearly every culture that we have to remember that its potency is not in its dramatic glamorization, but in its commonplace mundanity. It may not be a distant, high-powered executive or ostentatious predator, but someone much more familiar—perhaps even close and loved—who settles into a part of our lives in the most disturbing of ways. These people possess the same dualities of good and bad as we all do. They are not strangers; they are those we intimately know, those we work with, those we admire, and those we love. They must be shown the appropriate consequence and reprimand for their benefit as well. We cannot continue to perpetuate bad behavior through ignorance.

As a mother of three, I have had to embrace the difficult reality that one day my children may face extremely challenging encounters, some of them being unwanted sexual encounters. However, I am also hopeful. I feel that I am incredibly fortunate enough to bring my children up in this time where they will mature into a more socially conscious and compassionate society. While human nature may not change, culture certainly will, and they have the benefit of growing into a place where they will be a little less afraid to speak up against abuse.

If you too are a victim, or an individual who has been confided to about sexual abuse, let hope shine into your life. Allow it to enter your life and extend to other victims and survivors. Allow yourself to heal in a way that is truthful to yourself, not by anyone else's definitions. Asian Americans have to bear in mind that just because many of us are not willing to share our experiences or formally report them, it does not mean that we are any less affected and afflicted. Just because our stories are not known does not mean that we need to continue to live in the shadow of shame. I want both women and men, girls and boys in the Asian community to experience a time where sexual assault does not end in lasting shame and suppression. I want them to know that the shame is not to be carried by them, but by the perpetrator, an individual who will face appropriate reprimand. We need to disrupt this culture and create an environment that allows survivors to feel safe, heard, and believed.

Whether one chooses to share their story or not, I hope that they find peace with the past to find peace with themselves. For survivors, I know that it is a part of our personal history that never leaves us, but to let it have any authority over other realms of your life is to let it win. Allow yourself to be victorious. Allow yourself to be the hero of your own story.

Reflection

1. Have you experienced sexual assault? If so, how have you coped with the experience?
2. The church has not been supportive of sexual assault victims. How can the faith community engage in helping victims? What support can the church offer?
3. A sexual assault victim may experience shame, physical pain, and trauma. How can we all work towards alleviating people's pain and trauma?

MEMORY HAS NO STATUTE
OF LIMITATIONS

I praise you, for I am fearfully and wonderfully made.
Wonderful are your works; that I know very well.

—Psalm 139:14

There is a statute of limitations on prosecuting sexual crimes. But there is no time limitation on living with them.

When I was a child, I had my own encounter with sexual assault. I never reported it, and up to this point, I chose to tell only two people. A destructive idea we have about victims of sexual abuse or victims of abuse in general is that an unreported incident minimizes the victim's experience. There is a belief that if a victim really suffered at the hands of the abuser, they would have no other choice than to go to authorities about it. But that is simply not the case for the majority of sexual abuse survivors, and not reporting it doesn't make the suffering any less real. For myself, it is a truth of the past that never leaves me, and whether I chose to speak up during my youth, middle age, or old age, it was my own personal decision to do so. While some people need time to feel ready enough to talk about their experience and go through the lengthy and painful investigation process, others want to see justice almost immediately. This is completely up to the victim, and there is no right answer for how long one should wait, if they should wait at all, to speak up about it.

Time does not erase these memories; it may alter them, but they are certainly not forgotten. Time may adjust my feelings around this trauma, but I can strongly affirm all those who have chosen to live with it without disclosure. As a person of faith, I believe that the Spirit calls me to speak my truth regardless of what others may want of me. It also calls me to speak out the truth and challenge situations that reveal attempts to oppress the voices of other women. Uplifted by the #MeToo movement and recent news, I feel called to speak out against those who would seek to impose a statute of limitations on memory and truth-telling.

In 2018, when the news of Tom Brokaw's alleged sexual assault came to light, many thought that it was too old—that it had happened too long ago. They were upset that three women decided to speak up about it after all this time had gone by. The first to speak up was Linda Vester, a former war correspondent for NBC News, who described how Brokaw forced her to kiss him. Along with Peter Jennings at ABC News and Dan Rather at CBS News, Brokaw was one of the "Big Three" news anchors in the United States during the 1980s, 1990s, and early 2000s. He was a man of great prominence at NBC and, at the time, Vester was in a junior position. The bureaucratic power hierarchy that existed within the company was enough of a social barrier to keep her from speaking out. She was rising in her career; she had dreams of her own. Why risk it all for this incident? Why go against something far more powerful? For what?

She wasn't the only one who had this line of thought. Two other anonymous women spoke up about sexual misconduct against Brokaw. Brokaw denied these allegations, subsequently leading to 113 women signing a letter of support for Brokaw, including big names like Rachel Maddow and Andrea Mitchell. It has been reported that the lower staff workers at NBC felt pressured to sign the letter of support in protection of NBC, as Brokaw is synonymous with the network itself.

The letter does not change the truth; rather, it divulges how deeply and powerfully maintained the institution is in opposition to its members. Brokaw's garnering the support of 113 women he did not assault does not discount the numerous women he did abuse. Regardless of the number of women he assaulted or exploited, the accusations must still be met with the same vigilance shown for someone without his power or institutional support.

When a letter of support like that circulates in corroboration of an alleged perpetuator expressing statements like "man of tremendous decency and integrity" it signals to younger and less prominent women that speaking up is either futile or negated by those who should stand by in support. Further, it could send a message that, because Brokaw (or another "decent man") isn't still assaulting women, what he might have done decades ago when it was more socially commonplace is rendered irrelevant and forgivable. It indicates that just because a man didn't assault you personally, his assault of others is less valid. It dismisses the victim and suggests that their story may be less worthy and less relevant, or at least partially so. The force of the letter is in the 113 signatures and those women who were complicit in reinforcing the alleged actions of Brokaw.

We cannot defend some men and then condemn others who have committed similar assaults. We should defend those for whom there is no evidence and indict those whose acts are substantiated by fact. Why are we selectively defending some and not others? We have an obligation to listen, fairly judge all the evidence, prosecute objectively, and behave without prejudice. We must rethink the #MeToo movement and make sure it speaks for those who do not belong at the top of their bureaucracy.

Truth has no time limits. We should not disregard these three women who are finally standing up and sharing their long unshared experiences. We all have a moral imperative to be honest and circumspect when asked to support individuals under suspicion of wrongdoing. We need to fairly support those who have spoken up about abuse just as we honestly treat those accused. We need to support other women and men and pave the way for our children, friends, and neighbors so that attitudes regarding sexual crimes evolve and future victims will be unafraid to speak the truth in a court of law rather than the court of public opinion. In our lives, we must speak out the truth as we live the truth through faith. We need to speak out about oppression and act vigilantly against those seeking to impose a statute of limitations on memory and truth-telling.

Reflection

1. How do we begin to value each other and each other's physical beings?

2. How do we honor and respect each other?

3. Christianity emerged in the Greco-Roman world; therefore, Greco-Roman philosophy has inevitably influenced the Christian belief formations. Under its influence the notion of dualism became embedded. Dualism split the world, and part of the result was that the body was bad and the spirit was good. Consequently, the body has been negatively viewed and has been viewed as sinful. In our modern times, how can we change this negative view of the body?

LOVING OUR NEIGHBORS

For the whole law is summed up in a single commandment,
"You shall love your neighbor as yourself.

—*Galatians 5:14*

Since Donald Trump's inauguration in 2017, it seems as though the world has become much more divided, fragmented into groups and political sides that were not so pronounced before or, perhaps, so polarizing. It is not that Democrats and Progressives did not expect this to come about, but there was no way to prepare for the sight of colossal power in such unprepared hands. As I observe our reactions towards the Trump administration, I cannot help but mirror the feelings of disappointing regression. One of the first things that came to light under his administration, that first exhibited his severe rhetoric and irreverence, was a disturbing hatred towards immigrants and refugees. In his travel ban, he included seven Muslim-majority countries: Iraq, Syria, Iran, Sudan, Libya, Somalia, and Yemen were banned for 90 days, while he also suspended all refugees for 120 days. Trump is not holding a ban against Turkey, Saudi Arabia, Egypt, or Azerbaijan, where he has done business.

When we examine the history of our country, a ban against an ethnic group is not a novel idea. Asian American Pacific Islander immigration to the United States began in the mid-1800s. The annexation of California in 1846 by the United States opened the door to Asian laborers, with a significant wave of Chinese immigration during the California Gold Rush from 1848 to 1855. A series of restrictive laws were enacted that limited the life of Asians within the United States. In 1870, Congress passed a law that made Asian immigrants the only racial group barred from naturalization to United States citizenship.

Then came the Chinese Exclusion Act of 1882, which banned Chinese people from entering into the United States. In 1882, this Act was passed by Congress and signed by President Chester A. Arthur. It was a ten-year moratorium on Chinese labor immigration, and it became the first time that the U.S. government prevented an ethnic group from entering onto the U.S. soil.

The 1882 Chinese Exclusion Act not only prevented Chinese immigration, it placed new bans against the Chinese who already lived in the United States, as they had to obtain certifications to reenter the country if they ever left. This Act also denied citizenship to American-born children of Chinese immigrants even though the Fourteenth Amendment of 1870 granted citizenship to all children born in the United States. This was accomplished by Congress refusing the state and federal courts the right to grant citizenship to Chinese resident aliens. This meant that the courts could still deport them at any time, breaking up families and communities. When the Exclusion Act expired in 1892, Congress extended it for another ten years through the Geary Act. This act was made permanent in 1902, and it required each Chinese resident to register and obtain a certificate of residence. Without a certificate, they faced deportation.

This Geary Act regulated Chinese immigration until the 1920s. Chinese immigrants who were found without these certificates faced up to one year of hard labor followed by deportation. It was not until 1943 that Congress repealed the exclusion acts, leaving a yearly limit of 105 Chinese immigrants and giving foreign-born Chinese the right to seek naturalization. It was not until 1943 that Chinese were allowed to become U.S. citizens and were finally allowed to vote.

In addition, on February 19, 1942, President Franklin D. Roosevelt signed Executive Order 9066, which prescribed certain areas in the United States as military zones. This led to the transportation of Japanese Americans to internment camps, far from their homes on the Pacific coast. The conditions of these camps were undesirable and harsh. Some camps were built in former livestock pens with residual manure on the grounds. The walls of the buildings were often made of tarpaper, which provided little protection from the elements, making the winters extremely cold and the summers far too hot where the people lived. Armed soldiers guarded the camps, and barbed wire fences surrounded the compounds. Japanese Americans were interned, while Italian Americans and German Americans were not placed in camps during the war. Despite the United States being officially at war with these three countries, only the Japanese Americans were interned.

These discriminatory laws put into place by Congress tore families apart, creating mass turmoil, and they maintained disenfranchisement of those who were implicated. Asian Americans were commonly viewed as foreigners and not "real" Americans, their late citizenship acceptance among one of the reasons. They were viewed as the other. A form of this explicit racism that once was a part of the past has reemerged in far cruder expressions during the Trump era.

The first week of Trump's presidency had surpassed the expecta-tions of what Progressives and Democrats had prayed to be empty promises and frivolous entertainment. The statements made regard-ing the "ban of Muslims" has materialized in the most spiteful of ways. The racism that has always been embedded in America's fabric had been well concealed under the young, attractive, and progres-sive guise of Obama and his administration. But now it has bubbled to the surface yet again and made itself the central character in the national social and political landscape. It is not just the people close around us who experience its threatening effects, but those who watch from afar throughout the world. The influence is profound and extensive.

When European immigrants first came to the United States, they saw the Statue of Liberty. For decades, the Statue of Liberty has represented the virtue of American immigration, stating: "Give me your tired, your poor / Your huddled masses yearning to breathe free."[2] Perhaps this founding statement that brought the first immigrants together on the same land is the very testimony that will teach us how to treat our current immigrants.

We must reflect and remember our past so that we do not repeat it. Muslims and other immigrants or refugees alike have all retreated to this country for the same reasons that our ancestors did: hope and freedom. We need to become the beacon of light for those in search of that very thing, the people who come in search of a better life and in search of gracious opportunity. We can be that opportunity for others who come here full of hope; we can provide them the opportunity of communion and mutual support. This is the principle on which this country was built, and it is how we should define ourselves again.

Reflection

1. How do we work towards inclusion in society and in our churches?

2. How can we live out God's grace and extend it to those who are so different from us?

2. A section from Emma Lazarus's poem "The New Colossus."

CLIMATE CHANGE AND THE ECONOMY

The heavens are telling the glory of God;

and the firmament proclaims his handiwork.

—Psalm 19:1

One of the greatest tragedies of our present time is the way in which we have passively accepted economic gain from environmental destruction. We have always sustained ourselves with what we have found on earth. For as long as we have been here, we have survived on what was found around us: the water, arable earth, wind, vegetation, and animal life. At a certain point, we didn't intend just to survive off the land, but to thrive with one another using it. Our neighbors became extended, growing into quickly coalescing communities based on our extending mutual needs. We were able to generate our own value systems to support ourselves and others. We exchanged goods, livestock, and crops and assigned them a certain value to obtain other things required for more efficient and comfortable use of energy to make grain and agricultural goods. Once we progressed, the division of labor grew and people's needs and expertise were refined, thus bringing the distinction between the skilled laborer— the supplier—and their potential customer, who created demand.

This growth called for the employment of an element that was accommodating to all people, communities, and expanding markets: money. This is what began to connect the world like it never had been before.

In present times, when we think of the economy and the environmental crisis, we are quick to think of the corporation. We hold corporations accountable for their insistent efforts to convince consumers that their product, their message, and their value is separate from the reality of their operations. After all, according to the 2017 "Carbon Majors Report," more than 70 percent of the world's greenhouse gas emissions have been sourced from just one hundred companies since 1988. These are the companies that are producing the fossil fuels we use, the oil and gas companies that extract and market coal, natural gas, and oil. Major companies no doubt have a monumental role in driving climate change. While they are starting to make considerable efforts investing in clean energy, it may be too small and too late. The absolute strain between short-term profitability and crucial emissions reduction is what barricades them from considerable change. These top one hundred companies are in control of how their resources are withdrawn from the environment and marketed, but it is the consumers—we users—who sustain demand and burn the fossil fuels these companies produce.

We as consumers—individuals, households, businesses—must claim responsibility for pushing the carbon economy. The corporations will extract, generate, and market the fuels so that consumers can use them. Yet it is we who create carbon dioxide, whether resulting from frequent online shopping—producing shipping emissions from airplanes, trucks, and cars—or from using hot water, lights and other household utilities. The resources are distributed to us, and we feed back into the corporation and the cycle of damage.

Particularly in the context of the economy, we must remind ourselves that we are not just at a huge moral risk but a fiscal one. We have to move away from supporting the production of fossil fuels by urgently moving towards clean energy. The failure to find other sources of energy will be to everyone's detriment in the long term, as the resources will run out. Therefore, the money will as well.

Extreme weather has cost us $1.6 trillion since the 1980s in the United States alone. Forest fires, hurricanes, tornadoes, droughts, earthquakes, and extreme storms have had a huge economic and social impact on our country. Insurance firms are given permission to raise premiums to cover advancing costs from severe weather, which has slowly been making insurance too costly for many low- to middle-income families. The effects of lost belongings, destroyed homes, ravaged communities, and few solutions are immense; it cannot be fathomed by those who have yet to experience it. The prolonged recovery and lasting economic effect on severe weather–stricken individuals is enough to fracture the mind and break the spirit.

We ask ourselves, who will suffer the most from these economic and environmental disasters? The people who are already at risk, those who are already living in poverty, will lose the most on behalf of those who live in first-world comforts. These vulnerable communities continually go overlooked, and the effort to earn a living, uphold their families, and sustain their households will become more challenging each day. Food prices will rise as temperatures rise, and corn and soybean crops will plummet, making livestock feed more costly. This means animal products like dairy, poultry, and beef will diminish or become costly, reducing outdoor job employment and agricultural work, a primary source of work for many underprivileged communities around the world. The 3 billion people who are dependent on fish for main sources of protein are threatened. The global fish yields are steadily declining—the North Atlantic and Sea of Japan being at a decline of 35 percent in the past century, as many species are threatened with extinction.

We must keep in mind that while the environmental crisis may discriminate, our attempt at fighting it cannot. We must take charge of our destiny, of our actions, and of our progress. We can plant trees and stall deforestation—this is integral in creating oxygen and reducing carbon dioxide. There are many tree planting charities that one can donate to that give very poor communities work while rehabilitating their environment and its animal species. We can make an effort to become more carbon neutral by carpooling or changing our home appliances to those that are energy efficient or energy renewable; we can eat a more plant-based diet, reducing the methane, greenhouse gas, and carbon pollution used to transport animal products. The small choices we make now to consume less, waste less, and enjoy *more* will allow us to fully appreciate the things we have and, more importantly, the life we have.

Despite what some think, the real pursuit of saving the planet cannot be separated from addressing economic issues. This issue is embedded in everything in our world, intertwined and inclusive of all things: the tangible, like animal life, and the intangible, like our economy. Thus, we must remember that the ecological fight is not just directed or associated with the environment, but with the very health and survival of our global economy. We have to protect our most vulnerable economies. Creation must be saved and all of us need to take concrete actions. There must be serious plans for advocacy and theological engagement for any lasting changes to take root in our efforts to heal the earth.

Reflection

1. How are the economic and environmental issues related or intertwined?

2. The poor are the greatest victims of climate change. How can we work towards helping the poor, the marginalized, and the outcast in relation to climate change?

3. What did Jesus teach us about the poor and the suffering, and how does it correlate to relevant times of environmental crisis?

DEEP WOUNDS

The spirit of God has made me,

and the breath of the Almighty gives me life.

—Job 33:4

As a mother of three children in America, I constantly worry about the threat of a school or public shooting. Why must I brace them with the step-by-step procedures and behavioral conduct in the case of a school shooter? Why have I had to tell them, not once, but countless times that they need to pretend they are dead in such an absurdly recurrent threat? Why must I tell my children to keep vigilant? Why I must tell my children they are not endangered, when that affirmation is clearly flawed?

Schools are meant to be safe spaces for children, but rising numbers of public school shootings are indicative of the unsettling violence that prevails in America. The occurrence of gun violence in American schools continues to amplify.

Mass shootings are on the rise. In 2017, it was shocking for us to learn the initial reporting that twenty people had been killed in a public shooting in Las Vegas. Then the body count rose to fifty-nine people, the biggest mass shooting in U.S history thus far. Not only did we lose many lives, but hundreds were subjected to nearly fatal gunshot wounds. While I wish the shooting in Las Vegas would have led to gun law reform and improved firearm education, with the intense fiscal corruption and politicization of the arms industry, nothing improved.

The shooting in Las Vegas raised again the spectre of the gun lobby's complicity with mass shootings. Now you cannot play dead, because shots can come from above. Now we are forced to recognize that shots can come from a distance. Now you must realize that in this country a "quiet" or seemingly "normal" young white male can commit mass murder. We can no longer be on the lookout for certain "personality disorders" like that of Anders Behring Breivik, who killed eighty-six in Oslo in July 2011. Rather, we must consider the uncomfortable reality that the problems are founded on the failings of us—the adults, the parents, the politicians, the leaders, and the educators.

The senseless deaths and wounds inflicted on so many are deeply disturbing. Combined with the visceral horror of seeing and listening to such events unfold, these killings have led people to wonder for years, "How could this have happened?"

A few years ago, I was in Germany for a meeting. As we were being transported by bus from one city to another, our kind German leader told our group of world travelers, "You cannot understand Germany's love for speed on the road, just like we cannot understand America's love for guns."

This statement haunted me then and it feels even more disturbing to me now. The intimate political and gun affiliation has consciously allowed for senseless violence for the sake of "self-defense" and "protection." Growing up in Canada, I rarely heard of shootings of any sort; all the sensationalized stories of shootings came from one place and one place only—the United States. Our German guide voiced the opinion of many who live outside this country. Some countries have police officers who don't even carry guns;

Norway, Iceland, and Ireland are among them, and they display monumentally lower crime rates and gun-related deaths.

As Americans continue to argue that guns save lives, we need to reconsider and reflect on the unthinkable brutality that guns have inflicted on American soil. Studies show that Americans are ten times more likely to be killed by guns than are people in other developed countries.

Tragically, some may argue that our history of gun violence, experienced in the daily shootings not always covered by the media, are simply a cost for our firearms freedoms. There is a more peaceful, logical option; there can be a better future where our children can go to school without fear and where gun violence can be a thing of the past.

As more and more senseless tragedy haunts the streets, schools, homes, and public places of this country, we need to accept the reality that guns have only done the opposite of providing safety for their owners—they have heightened the violence, danger, and risk of those around them. We must expunge our irrational loyalty and belief in guns, if not for ourselves, then for our children.

Reflection

1. How can we work towards overcoming gun violence in our society, schools, and neighborhoods?

2. What local, state, and federal actions can we be involved in to fight against gun violence?

CARE FOR THE WHOLE CREATION

> But ask the animals, and they will teach you; the birds of
> the air, and they will tell you; ask the plants of the earth,
> and they will teach you; and the fish of the sea will declare
> to you. Who among all these does not know that the hand
> of the Lord has done this? In his hand is the life of every
> living thing and the breath of every human being.
>
> —*Job 12:7–10*

I have a reoccurring dream. It begins with me in a black, nebulous space. My feet are muffled on soft ground. I start to walk forward. Without direction, I walk with no sense of time—I have no place to be and no place to go. I see a white door emerge from darkness. When I go to knock on the door, no one answers. I knock again, but no response. The third time I knock, the door nudges open. Tropical air. The sound of cicadas, birds, and running water fills the silence. Through the door the world that materializes around me is one of perfect beauty. There is untouched earth, and strange animals wander all around, most of which I have never seen before and some of which do not exist at all. Opulent emerald plants tangle and soar, and on the ground, a thick root edges under my foot. I follow the root until I reach a trunk; my eyes follow it all the way up. A totemic tree stands before me, bearing the hanging gems of every conceivable fruit. I do not need to keep wandering; I have no need to wander. I take a seat against the trunk without thought of ever getting up again. Then, I reach for a plum above my head.

I have never been a vivid dreamer, so it surprises me that not only do I have this one, extremely evocative dream, but I have had it recur ever since I started to become more invested, or rather, more desperate about the state of climate change.

When I awaken, I feel robbed of a utopia. I feel as though I really lived this dream, and that I really lost it. But the more I think about it and continue to have this dream, the more I start to believe that this isn't just a dream I lost, but a lost reality created by my subconscious mind.

Today's climate is different from that of my childhood—and certainly antithetical to this dream. I can feel the difference. As we see the climate changing in our lifetime, we need to think more seriously about how we are going to stop this from deepening into further devastation. Without change, our current lifetime and all future generations will suffer unimaginable consequences. The weakest and the poorest are affected by the hedonistic and greedy behaviors of high-consumption lifestyles that are the norm in the first world, especially in the United States. Due to our self-indulgence, we have gone down the path of self-destruction. If we are to make any inroad into this human rights issue, we must tackle the issue of climate change immediately.

We have bought into the false notion that nothing will run out. Dr. Jeffrey Sachs, director of Columbia University's the Earth Institute, said we cannot keep believing the earth is a "supermarket." Such a view has convinced us of our sustained human centrality, to not worry about resources, believing there will always be more for us to consume without repercussions. Many still believe that the threat of scarcity is false and that we will continue to have what we want, where we want, as long as we have the capacity, the money, and the resources to obtain it.

The mention of climate change brings division. We introduce debate from those in the realms of science, economics, theology, sociology, politics, media, and the arts to dispute amongst themselves and amongst one another. Theology and politics have been significant long-standing players in this dialogue.

The bond between the two has been purposefully engineered and upheld over periods of heightened tension on matters of race, gender, and, now, the environment, to a point where the main predicator of support against climate change is political stance. It seems that the issue is easily relegated to politics because it carries so much weight, controversy, and complexity in the individual mind. At this crucial time in history, we must realize that climate change is not a belief system, an elitist concern, or a political debate topic. We know that the planet's climate is at a turning point and that it will lead to decimating the earth's resources regardless of conflicting understanding. When we relate ourselves to our current observations in nature with proven facts and scientific data, we see that all creation is under attack. Climate change is an effect of the growing human environmental impact, which is why natural disasters, pollution, biodiversity reduction, species extinction, and habitat fragmentation continue to worsen.

We must acknowledge that climate change will hit hardest for the very people whom we are urged to look after the most, escalating poverty, hunger, and illness in many of the communities that are already heavily afflicted. It will reduce the natural and human resources and lead to major political instability and aggravate the refugee crises. The current effect is real. We do not need to argue about the validity at this point, as we can see the suffering in every connecting strand of life. Thus, we must remember that God's love has been shared in our hearts so that it can be shared with others;

the love we have is the love we give to our sisters and brothers around the globe who suffer at the feet of this issue. If not for ourselves, we must do it for the people who are at the highest risk—there is no time to resist acting on this issue.

So much of this resistance—resistance that comes from all people, from all beliefs—is birthed from the same place: fear. We fear the insurmountable losses: our way of life, our customary patterns, our dreams for the future, our comforts, our ignorance. We are lost in fear and remain stagnant, paralyzed, guilty, and anxious. This is why so many of us have had climate change on our radar for some time now but have taken so long to act upon it. Perhaps it seems so grand and so far out of our reach that we end up pushing it aside because we lack faith in individual power. But people who make it a mission to live their lives more consciously, compassionately, and openly about this cause make the difference. It doesn't take power as much as it takes strength.

Now that it is becoming impossible to ignore, many people are being prompted to act based on fear alone. We see the headlines, we see the effects, and we understand the grave impact on the future. But moving forward, we must try and find motivation outside of fear alone. Fear is not what will sustain us and give us hope, as it is not from God. Rather, we should feel empowered and hopeful, for we have the strength of the spirit; this strength gives us compassion for those who are suffering, underprivileged, and less fortunate than us. We are motivated by compassion and hope for these people, for the creatures and life of the earth, and for the earth that is under attack, both now and in the coming times.

We all live on the same planet. As we cohabit the world with each other, we are reminded of our mutual responsibility to protect, care, and live for the whole of creation: the entirety of animal and human life, and the air, water, and earth of the natural world. While I cannot return to the world of my dreams where I only have to open a door to rediscover the plenum of life and resource, I can turn and see the small patches of unmarred beauty in our real world, where untouched earth bears all the life and nutrients we could ever need. It is a reminder that there are still affirmations of hope in our circumstances and paragons of God's creation.

Reflection

1. How can we move towards climate justice as individuals, families, and churches?

2. What are you doing currently to live more sustainably? How can you share these practices with others?

LISTENING TO
INDIGENOUS VOICES

If it is possible, so far as it depends on you,

live peaceably with all.

—*Romans 12:18*

When we are young, we look ahead of our lives believing that time will pause for us. We find ourselves shaded in the glory of youth, looking at ourselves in the mirror thinking that life might just hold on and let us remain the same. We breathe, eat, walk, learn, cry, work, pray, and sleep in these young bodies of ours—and then suddenly, as if we had blinked for too long, we are not so young anymore. We realize after yet another ordinary day of looking in the mirror, that something has changed, it has changed all along, and we may have fewer years ahead than those that have passed. Ultimately, time was not as slow as we once thought it to be.

For many of us, our daily consciousness of aging is like our daily consciousness of the earth. Most of us don't feel like we are in positions of denial in our connection to our earth; rather, we feel vastly distant from it. We see our faces every day and don't notice the slow change; within our insulated cities, suburbs, residential streets, and superstores, we do not get a visceral sense of how far we humans have dominated the earth and just how much it has changed. Despite our assuming possession of our environment and then demolishing it for our personal capital and human development, we display limited awareness or accountability for its demise. Most of us do not see much of this earth in our lifetimes. We cannot but help to make this irrevocable home of ours a mere stranger.

Like our bodies, our planetary home does not hold out for us. It does not remain unchanged over time. It ages; it bears life; it is fallible; it becomes fragile—and despite the reality that it is devastating to all life, we continue to weaken it by our own accord.

The health of our earth is waning, and all life on earth that fails as a result is because of us. It is not just an isolated being that will be affected in the course of one lifespan, but all corporeal things on earth thereafter.

It is easy to cynically convince ourselves that nothing can be done, but this is precisely the attitude that has led us to this disaster in the first place. It is with human apathy, greed, and ignorance that the earth has gone awry, and it will most certainly fight back in the most ruinous of ways. What will come will be the greatest disaster that civilization will encounter: the collapse of our planet.

As a result, we have no choice. We need to mobilize now, we need to plan for today, we need to have proactive conversations for the future. Real change begins small; it begins with a single thought that matures into action, action that is exposed to another being who transforms their actions as well. We must grapple with the notion that we are leaders to countless others in our lives, and that our influence is far more extensive than we may believe.

Christians are integral in this battle. We have once understood ourselves as the highest form of God's creation. In this self-exalted role, we have dominated the earth and all its life, creating havoc on the planet. Guided by our imposed primacy and ideology, Christians were greatly responsible for rationalizing the capitalization of the environment for false defenses of morality. We went far beyond our need-based use to explicit exploitation to satisfy our insatiable desire for attainment.

Moving forward, we must take responsibility. We cannot repeat the behavior that has now become the norm. We cannot rely on ourselves in this change. This is a revolution of behavior for the entirety of our species. Thus, we have to congregate. We must be active in coalition. We have to be willing to look to others who are taking action.

Members of the Working Group on Climate Change (WCC) met in Taiwan in June 2019 to strategize for the future and establish the forthcoming work that pursues the slowing of climate change and fortifying methods for climate justice. This work is going to be implemented on a domestic and global scale. This was the first time that the working group also met with the WCC's Indigenous Peoples' Programme Reference Group to explore how the two groups can work in union to achieve common goals. The Reference Group seeks to create transcendent community networks, advocate for Indigenous peoples' rights, and raise awareness of Indigenous peoples' spiritualities and theologies.

As the meeting proceeded, it became clear that we cannot fight against climate change without the involvement of Indigenous peoples. Members of the Reference Group reminded us that the Indigenous peoples have been fighting climate change since before the beginning of colonization. They have valuable experience combatting governments, corporate power, and modern threats that continue to invade and pollute their land and abuse stolen resources to the extreme.

Indigenous groups have long been calling governments, religious groups, and communities to work together to stabilize the climate and attain justice for their abused land. Furthermore, Indigenous groups are the demographic most affected by climate change, as many of these communities are agricultural rather than industrial. Since the colonization of their land, they have been exploited by European settlers who captured their lands and worked to erase them not just as a culture, but as a civilization through genocide, rape, and assimilation. This colonialism has facilitated and encouraged large corporations to expropriate and exploit indigenous land while heavily polluting the surrounding environment, proximally near and distant. Indigenous peoples have told us for years about the nature of this destruction, and now that it has begun to have a terrible effect in our lives, we are finally willing to take notice.

A global point of view must gather many different experiences and arrive at a common voice and approach. Analysts of imperialism need to take heed of these integral Indigenous voices. They have a holistic understanding of climate justice as they relate the environment with spirituality itself, a way of thinking that has been trivialized by the rest of the world. Indigenous peoples cannot divorce the present-day land from the land of their ancestors, as their ancestors' spirits roam the land with its peoples, conversing with them, and guiding them. They remind us that the spirit exists within all things and that all life on earth often embodies a spiritual aspect, making its preservation equitable in value to that of human lives. Unlike most other human populations, Indigenous peoples do not regard themselves as the center of the earth's ecosystem or of life itself. They are merely a part of it, a life that moves through time momentarily giving and taking from the world with grace.

Indigenous groups remind us of the interconnectedness of spirit and nature. Christianity rejected this idea in favor of dualism, a divide between spirit and body or between spirit and the natural world. This divide has had consequences, as Christians continued to state that the body nature is bad and the spirit is good without ever seeing the interconnectedness of the spirit—the notion that the body/nature and spirit are actually one. We have neglected to see the spirit as part of the natural world. While animism or shamanism had hinted at such an understanding, Christians viewed these ideas as heathen mistakes. This divide has had negative consequences for the natural world. We have forgotten and denied that the Spirit of God the Creator resides in all of creation and taking care of creation demands priority. We need to incorporate this understanding and move away from dualism. This will help us understand how we can be part of the solution of climate change.

This understanding connects us to land and spirit. It incites us to reevaluate the rules of the household so that we can respect one another and all of creation; we do this in the hope of living together in a world less pained and in a world less conflicted. It reminds us that equity and respect for all creation is required for the necessary transformation of humanity by the Spirit. It reminds us that all life is precious, and all faith communities must stand in solidarity with Indigenous groups who are at the frontlines of the climate change battle.

Indigenous peoples remind us that spirituality comes from the natural world, a place that encompasses all we need—the water, land, air, and all that lives therein. On behalf of Indigenous peoples, the forgotten peoples, the first peoples, we need to heed their call to save the planet. The two groups, the Working Group on Climate Change and the Indigenous Peoples' Programme Reference Group of the WCC, should find agency to build a stronger community and channel of communication to work for climate justice. Together, we need to continue to advocate for policies that protect the planet and be challengers of powerful institutions and corporations that profit from environmental exploration and destruction.

We cannot be oblivious to the Indigenous peoples who have continually contested and writhed at the sight of our actions on creation. We cannot turn away from the reality of vanishing species among the animals with whom we share this planet. We cannot ignore the respondent cries coming from the earth, manifested in mega-storms, severe droughts, rising sea levels, melting icebergs, increasing temperatures, and deadly forest fires. We need to heed these warnings and move towards sustainable, conscious lifestyles and proactive education that respects God's creation, uplifts Indigenous peoples' rights, and embraces the life-giving spirit that resounds through all creation.

Reflection

1. We must be proactive and fight back against corporations and big companies who are polluting the earth. How can we start to fight back?

2. How can faith communities fight back against climate change?

LIVING IN RELATIONSHIP

Peace seems to be an anomaly in most of our lives. The truth is that we are born into a mind of conflict and a world of discord, lived out in intimate relationship with those we call loved ones and those we call enemies. Conflict is part of what motivates us to act rather than remain stagnant in our lifelong search for fulfillment, meaning, and lasting joy. However, many of us are often rendered hopeless by the impermanence or absence of such things within ourselves and within our relationships. The world at large has always rested on this predicament, never finding stability and contentment in the present. We have been taught to energize ourselves with a hunger for greater future esteem despite the fact that we ordinarily attain it at the cost of others. We fall into battle over our perceived differences: our race, our sex, our status, our religions, our politics, our social beliefs, and our land. Whether it stems from greed or individual superiority, we humans regularly go through unnecessary conflict for personal gain.

Like many of us, I was born into an environment of world conflict that took its toll on the possibility of hopeful relationship. In the late 1960s of South Korea, the tensions between the North and South were highly strained. The war had not been over for long, and the economic and social ramifications were strong in my very early years of life before my family emigrated to Canada. I was only a baby when

I first sat in front of the televised news that covered the hysteria about and abhorrence of our North Korean half. I was quick to be reminded all my adolescent life that North Koreans were all born into bodies of corruption and were willfully complicit with a malicious authoritarian government. I was fed with fanatical threats that we were always a step away from war and mass genocide and that I should carry a practical level of fear as a safeguard.

Of course, living this way is not uncommon for many people in the world. At any given period, political and social conflicts pervade our perspectives and relationships. In the current government, conflict barrages the daily lives of millions of Americans. In war-torn Iraq, Syria, Yemen, Sudan, or Ukraine, people live under political, religious, and social terror. Especially as members of the church, we have to acknowledge our own potential contribution to human division and broken relationships. Religion has been one of the most significant forces of bloodshed, and we need to be vigilant in our attempts at reconciling the horrors that afflict us. We people of faith have committed—and continue to commit—a long history of violence and war.

People of faith should not think themselves different from any other. The drives of fear and hunger in human nature do not escape us. But can we concede to those drives? Is it enough to speak ill of them and call ourselves moral because we are not the chief perpetrators? Can we relieve ourselves of our own potential fault through trivial deference?

While we do not have the capacity or responsibility to confront all the corruptions of the world, we all have to admit that we concede to some of the battles that exist more intimately to us. All of us have a hand in some wrong in the world, in the brokenness of relationship and the strain of peace, as we are fallible and flawed beings. Our internal states are always pushed to the edge of unrest and dissatisfaction, so the peace we let in and show ourselves, the peace we demand for ourselves, must not simply exist and die on its own. It must not only suffuse us with satisfaction but permeate all the connections between us and the conflicted souls around us in order to bring higher justice to the world. Extending peace offers us all an inner source of refuge and a life of hope.

We must remember, however, that hope is not the solution. The mind of conflict, the world of discord, will not recover through our hope alone. As we remember that hope is anchored to the very presence of God, the "inner place" that resides in all of us, we must find restoration from God to allow the remedy of hope to bring healing between us—individually and collectively. We must take action. We must be vigilant. We must begin discussions with family, friends, and church and continue to engage the current and impeding conditions that divide us. This is not a social issue; this is not a political issue; this is not an economic issue; this is an all-encompassing living issue that transcends us and all we know on earth if we are to know peace. We have so much to work towards, and, thus, so much to hope for.

BUILDING HEALTHY RELATIONSHIPS

For where two or three are gathered in my name,
I am there among them.

—Matthew 18:20

From the moment we enter this world we are bound to another being. We emerge with a predetermined relationship to our circumstances, our body, our mind, our environment, and our family. Those who give us life, our parents, often bear the earliest foundation for human connection in our lifetimes, forming our first conscious experience of what it means to relate to another being. Once our inaugural parental relationship expands, it informs our networks of relations with others: our extended family, friends, and eventually, our partners.

As social beings, the inextricable ties we have to other people are what have historically allowed us to survive. We formed tribes, communities, villages, and nations that lent us safety, identity, and a sense of belonging. Relationships have not changed since then. We rely on one another. We rely on connections and communities. This fundamental necessity is often what provides us our greatest joys and fulfillments in life and also our most profound suffering. Why so many of our relationships are strained and end up collapsing should be no surprise. It is certainly not a mark of failure, but a designation of our own microcosmic chaos and complexity. Humans are complicated enough as we are, and adding another person to the mix to form a relationship creates a separate being unto itself. A relationship is akin to a life, with its inception, growth, and decline. With new digital advancements, we have been given more options with the beginning part—the inceptions—as social networks, online dating, and meet-up apps have established new ways of creating relationships and rekindling old ones. But we are still fettered to the same unavoidable problems with maintaining relationships; perhaps technology has only exacerbated the complications. This part of the formula has not been figured out yet. It is still up to us.

In my house, as I know is true with many other families, we text each other even if we are in the next room. It's convenient. When I don't want to commit the time it takes to make a phone call to a family member or a friend, I might simply send a three- or four-word text to initiate conversation. It might be something like, "hi are u there," or "what r u doing." It sounds curt, but I know that the reality of my attempts at communicating parallels many of our attempts at communicating and even maintaining relationships. We try and take convenient approaches, the ones that require the least amount of effort for the reward. A text rather than a phone call; a phone call rather than a face-to-face conversation; a surface conversation rather than a conflict; a conflict rather than a dialogue. I know that many of us stay on the surface of safety, ignoring the negative and embracing the positive, but if we continue this pattern the central problems we fear grow closer to becoming the center of the relationship.

Think of your troubled, broken, or lost relationships. Whether it be a past lover, a parent, a child, or a friend, those whom we care about disappoint us, as we do them. Those we are in relationships with become a part of us, and we do everything we can to preserve ourselves when they are no longer in our lives the way they once were. We suffer and hold onto the other in our minds until we are hanging by the last thread. When it comes to this point, we let go and experience loss, grieving the relationship as if we lost a life— and in essence we have. Because, simply, we love, and thus we suffer.

We have to welcome pain. We have to accept it as an essential component to being connected to another. That is why, when we are in a place of pain or disruption in our relationships, the maintenance of hope will give us strength. But we must be present in our relationships, otherwise such hope will not thrive. Hope does not bridge gaps between lands, it calls for the land to unify. So while we slide further into the ease of physical detachment, we have to hold onto the one thing whose worth cannot be exchanged. We need to try to cultivate and tend to our relationships despite inconvenience, pain, or even futility. We must try. Being intentional and actively trying to be in physical spaces with one's spouse, family, friends, and faith community is essential to sustaining and building healthy relationships in a world relying increasingly on indirect avenues of connection.

However radically our environment changes, and however much culture changes, God remains. God is not subject to the frailties and waverings of human relationships; rather, God provides us with steadfast support and hope through all of time. Christ puts emphasis on relationships and says that when two or more are gathered, Christ is there. Thus, when we put Christ center in our relationships so that Christ can be centered in all that we do, we will progress as individuals, evolve as partners, and flourish as believers.

Reflection

1. What are your most difficult relationships?

2. What are some ways you can better difficult relationships?

3. In the busyness of life, we often neglect our spiritual relationship with God. How do you nurture your spiritual growth and relationship with God?

VULNERABILITY AND PARENTHOOD

> But he said to me, "My grace is sufficient for you, for power
> is made perfect in weakness." So, I will boast all the more
> gladly of my weaknesses, so that the power of Christ may
> dwell in me. Therefore, I am content with weaknesses,
> insults, hardships, persecutions, and calamities for the sake
> of Christ; for whenever I am weak, then I am strong.
>
> —2 Corinthians 12:9-10

After his first year of college, my oldest son did his first internship in Charlotte, North Carolina. It was hard to have him away from home; he had been back for only a few days in the summer after his classes ended at college before he left for this new opportunity. Then, after a summer in Charlotte, he returned home for two days before he left to begin his sophomore year. Needless to say, it was an emotionally difficult time for me. I had always imagined that sending my kid off to college would be a joyous event, a catharsis of sorts, but I surprised myself with the tumultuous emotions of "letting go."

Sending my first child off sent me on a retrospective look at my life as a mother. I am still trying, as I now have two in college, to understand what it means to be vulnerable in this role. As I see it, embracing vulnerability is a feminist act because it resists the stereotype of the self-contained mother who continually sacrifices without any self-regard. While it requires a commitment to care for the self, it also acknowledges that the self is always in relation with others. It identifies that the self cannot be made invulnerable through meritocracy, something institutions often fail to recognize; rather, it can be a place of theological reflection and solidarity.

It seems that now my vulnerability stems from the feeling of inadequacy that has always followed me in the process of raising my kids—many mothers can relate to such a feeling. As a mother of two teenage children and one young adult, I have always done what I could to raise them. However, in my own busyness of being a professor, it feels as though I have not been there as much as I should have been, and that I fall short of my own expectations. One day, I feel like I am doing such a good job, and then the next day—when I lose my cool with the kids and spiral into a senseless argument or fight—I feel totally frustrated and incompetent. As parents, we work tirelessly, albeit imperfectly, to get things done at home the way we see fit. But at the end of the day, we will always inevitably have questions about why we do what we do.

In those times, I feel at my most vulnerable and perhaps my most insecure. This is a feeling that not only comes to me at home but also at work. I have felt that there have been many instances where I could not keep up with the demands in both places. As an Asian American woman, I am followed by the social expectancy of astounding success; I often feel that I am overcompensating to excel at home and at work to prove to myself that I have an equal footing to my counterparts and that I am worthy of sharing space in the academic and theological realm—and then I ultimately realize that my home life has been pushed to the back burner and I question if any of it was worth it at all. Most of the time, I find myself turning to a state of stoicism instead of situating myself in the challenging hands of vulnerability. In these times, we have to give ourselves the chance to be vulnerable as we open ourselves up and see ourselves as we are. We see ourselves in our most fearful form; we see the failures that we have made or have caused, often projecting failures that have not even occurred yet; we see the mistakes that we have made and are currently making; we contemplate these decisions and agonize over our regrets and wish that we could have done something differently. As we remain lodged in these vulnerable places, we have to confront this darker part of ourselves and learn that the time spent toiling on our mistakes is futile. It does not lead to the alteration of the mistake or its repercussions, but keeps us in a deepening hole of regret and discontent. The only thing that we can do is make meaningful progress and learn from the experiences, taking them as they are: a part of our life story and a part of our journey to self-knowledge.

As I ascend deeper in the crux of vulnerable motherhood, I always try to seek a way out. I see the loose ends of ropes that I can never quite reach to lift myself out—and I stay there. We have been primed to believe that accepting our shortcomings is something to be curtailed and avoided, and I am the first to admit how complicit I am in this. But we have to embrace that vulnerability simply means letting our guard down. Vulnerability is an admission to our participation in an imperfect world. We are not the supermoms, or in my case, the tiger-moms, that society poses us as. We cannot always cook homemade meals. We cannot sew up all those lost buttons that keep falling off pants and shirts. We cannot make every soccer game, every dance recital, or every competition. We cannot do everything at home and at work. And it is okay to accept these fated shortcomings and invest our limited time into places that may need it more than others. It is not a sacrifice, but a delicate attempt at finding stability across all our responsibilities.

When I was giving birth to my third child in Toronto, SARS had broken out in the city. My hospital was shut down for weeks, so they instructed those giving birth to call a number once the contractions began so that they could direct them to an open hospital. I was sent to one of these hospitals. What followed was not at all in the same vein as my previous two birthing experiences. It was not the coddling, sweet, awe-filled environment of the past. For my first two deliveries, my doctor had turned me over onto my left hip and administered an epidural. For my third delivery, this was not the case. The pain that I endured without medical alleviation was unparalleled. My labor lasted eight hours. I writhed in pain for the entirety of it, while also wondering if something was fatally wrong during the last half. I thought at that moment, "This is it! I am going to die; give me an epidural!" I was in unrelenting torment, it felt like someone was slowly pulling my left leg off, and my eyes began rolling up into my head. The interning doctor that aided me refused to give me an epidural without any apparent reason. I had desperately needed it for my first two births, as I have a hairline fracture on my left hip from my twenties that was extremely painful during delivery.

This pain makes sense because when my baby was born, he was a whopping 9 pounds, 1 ounce—a huge baby with a huge head. I couldn't believe the size of this newborn. He looked like he was already three months old!

The next morning, as I walked around the hospital floor looking for the nurse, another new mom who had heard me screaming in childbirth said to me, "You don't have to be a superwoman. You could have asked for help!" I asked, "Did you? Did you get an epidural?" She said yes, and in that moment, I felt that my doctor had personally, bitterly betrayed me. However, in retrospect, this experience illuminates a wider problem, where women undergo the obligations of certain pains while also being undermined for speaking up about it. In my opinion, my doctors were largely responsible for my unnecessary, prolonged agony, forcing me to take on the "superwoman" position. Inadvertently, I was made to perform this role for others, contributing and further reinforcing the notion of the "superwoman complex," which tells us that without protest or question, we have to do it all. But clearly, we cannot. Throughout our lives, women are conditioned to endure pain silently. Our limits, our moments of weakness, our regrets, and our downfalls should not be dismissed, but recognized.

Contrary to how we may feel, this is the pursuit of liberated solidarity: we either can break down and wallow in our failure, or we can step into our vulnerable spaces and ask for help. When we become vulnerable, we allow our weaknesses to show and let others know that we cannot do it alone. We express to our community that we need help and that we need each other to survive. We recognize that we cannot raise a child by ourselves and that we need the goodness, strength, and help of the community to bring a child into this world and raise it in the hands of shared, conscious responsibility.

As such, this can be a place of theological reflection and support: Vulnerability is an avenue for help, hope, grace, and love. We must allow ourselves to become more vulnerable, and once we experience the power of this openness and this exposition, we can allow ourselves to be truly honest and accept all the genuine brokenness of others. Through this compassion, we can even get a glimpse of the Divine, who stands in solidarity with the vulnerable. The passion narrative shows Christ's vulnerability to the world. Vulnerability then becomes a theological exercise and mode of living. Vulnerability is necessary, saving, and gracious, giving us unified courage and understanding of our joint human experience.

Reflection

1. In what ways was Jesus vulnerable? What does Jesus' vulnerability teach us?

2. How does vulnerability open us up to God's will?

3. How can we grow in our vulnerability to serve God?

WALKING HAND IN HAND

Train children in the right way,
and when old, they will not stray.

—Proverbs 22:6

There is no greater agony than bearing
an untold story inside you.

—Maya Angelou, I Know Why the Caged Bird Sings

The written word is a powerful source of change. Many of us know of works of writing through characters. Well-written characters offer us readers a piece of ourselves; our humanity is reflected through storied tension and relationships. Through story we achieve the distillation of experiences far from our own. It moves worlds, lives, and minds, drawing us out of our small realities and bringing us into a new one, imagined and true—in fiction, the imagined is the truth. The imagined allows both the writer and the reader to experience life through different skins, times, circumstances, and worlds. The truths in writing, both the act of it and the consumption, compel us to think differently. Radically shifting our worldview and our empathetic capacities towards a higher good, good writing challenges us, but at best, it changes us. It evolves our limited human experience to one that can be attuned to a greater, universal one.

As tedious and anxiety-inducing as writing can be, it has been necessary for me. Years ago, when I decided to co-write a book with my daughter, I knew that I would be taking on a significant challenge. The topics and people in the book would be difficult to write about, as I would have to greatly spare emotional subjectivity while remaining constructive and honest. I would have to write about myself and my daughter, while she wrote about herself and me.

Co-writing in itself is difficult, but to do it with someone as close as a family member is even harder. It is deeply personal and emotional, and thus more likely to cause conflict.

The aim for the book was to represent both my immigrant perspective and my daughter's as a child of an immigrant seeking to make sense of her Korean heritage. It became a cross-generational dialogue between my daughter and me on family, race, faith, relationships, and loss. I sought to share the perspectives of a mother and daughter on issues that are both intimate and social, to shed light on female perspectives from two different stages of life from two different periods of upbringing.

Writing this book took the span of three years. From the beginning to the end, my daughter went from middle school to high school, which made both the process and the work significant to her upbringing. It lived with her for a consequential part of her life, the prime of her adolescence, so I was acutely aware of the potential impacts it would have on her.

What if the process was disastrous and she would look back begrudgingly? What if she hated the final book and acknowledged it with a guise of indifference, or even worse, mortification? What if this would turn out to be a completely avoidable vexation that would turn our relationship sour? I thought all those things through time and time again, but I knew that whatever insecurities I had at the time would be overturned by the opportunity to create something meaningful for the both of us. It would be an opportunity to mature alongside one another, challenge one another, and learn from the other's experience.

Pitching and convincing the project to my daughter was the easy part; the difficult part was convincing her to do the work after her initial head of steam. In the duration of the writing process, it took a lot of me asking, arguing, and even begging her to do her part. From the beginning moments of starting this project, I knew that it would take at least two to three years. When a project takes several years to complete, the work permeates your life so deeply that it simply becomes synonymous with living. That is what happened with that book. It figuratively and physically became a part of our lives. I would look at her across the kitchen table without saying a word and she would respond to a question I had for her about her writing. She would knock on my bedroom door at night and I would supply her with a series of comments and answers to queries unasked. It embedded itself into our daily discourse and manifested into innumerable piles of paper, stacked like a cityscape around the house: in my bedroom corner, in her dresser drawers, on our kitchen table, and on our hoarding chair of papers and research documents. It transformed our home into a space of jot-notes and sprawled over, scribbled pages of rough drafts. So to say this project was pervasive is an understatement. From the beginning, I held onto the hope that this project would see an end, but as time went on, the end seemed to become more and more elusive.

Trying to maintain any role as a mother and scholar had already come with plenty of challenges, but one of the many advantages of learning to harmonize this balance was the opportunity to communicate more with my daughter. Mothers and daughters bear an extremely special relationship. Though tense at times, these relationships hold the promise of becoming one of the most empowering and nurturing connections made between two people. We went through periods of fervent action, tension, and quiet stillness while we spent time together. It felt like the book wedged itself between us at times, and often I wondered whether it brought us union or divide.

But the writing process drew us together as we were able to discuss, reflect, and write about what was important in our hearts. We touched on subjects of sustaining meaningful friendships, building strong marriages, reflecting on our Christian faith, and working towards a just society. As we tackled these issues in our book, we started to tackle justice, or rather, its attainment, in our own home as we worked together. We recognize that building healthy families strengthens our communities and our society. It is my belief that the network of the family sustains the backbone of thriving communities, and in order to build and sustain peaceful societies, we must begin practicing justice in our homes.

Writing this book together allowed me to learn from my daughter, but also, it allowed me to learn how to find and rediscover hope in stillness. This is when hope seems most precious to us. All throughout those years, when we both periodically stopped writing, I thought the project would never be completed. But it was in those moments when one of us felt like giving up that the other found clarity and purpose to continue through hope. With encouragement from each other, collaboration, dedication, and commitment to sharing our stories, we were able to finish our book, offering it as a source of encouragement, joy, and love to those in our community and beyond. I learned again that the journey rather than the end, the writing rather than the book, is the part of our individual story that gives us opportunity to live out our imagination and exalt our triumphs to their most meaningful potential. In all our pursuits, and in all our journeys, let us find life-giving hope along the way to enrich the vital relationships that will provide us with the fulfillment and love that we need.

Reflection

1. How is your relationship with your parents or your children? Have you taken on a project together to learn and grow together? If so, how did it go?

2. Family relationships are full of changes, negotiations, and growth. How can you better nurture your family relationships?

WHAT TAYLOR SWIFT'S
BREAKUPS TEACH US

> Let your steadfast love become my comfort
> according to your promise to your servant.
>
> *—Psalm 119:76*

I often turn to my children in an effort to understand popular culture. I frequently ask them who is considered relevant and significant in music at the moment, as I feel that celebrity is one of the most accurate ways to gauge current culture. While I can understand certain people like Adele, Nicki Minaj, and Kendrick Lamar, none mystify me more than Taylor Swift. I ask my children why she has remained so popular and beloved, and even they admit they don't really know. I don't get it. Why has she remained so popular, to the point where, according to Lisa Respers' CNN article, "Taylor Swift takes over the world."[3]

To me Taylor Swift has never seemed to be a particularly strong singer, dancer, performer, or even memorable personality. While there

3. Lisa Respers France, "Taylor Swift takes over the world," CNN.com, 11/14/2014, https://www.cnn.com/2014/11/06/showbiz/celebrity-news-gossip/taylor-swift/index.html, accessed July 31, 2018.

is a myriad of other talented artists residing in neighboring heights of fame and success to Taylor Swift, none have reached her formidable, lasting position at the top of the industry. There are others in my family who share my opposition to Swift, also attesting that her popularity seems disproportionate to her likability as an artist. Without going further into arbitrary talent or artistic integrity, it is worthy to evaluate what her impenetrable relevance brings to light. It must mean something for her influence in popular culture to be so strong.

So what is the attraction of Taylor Swift? I think there is something to be said about her notoriety as a prolific dater, which is what first throttled her into the position of a being a tabloid favorite. Public female figures known to date frequently, even quickly, around the echelons of power or public prominence will likely find themselves under a plethora of scrutinizing opinions. Being known for her highly publicized breakups has actually helped her career. Some say that no publicity is bad publicity, and for Ms. Swift it seems to be true. She uses her celebrity and the very fame of a relationship's collapse as emotional content for her songs of young heartbreak, romantic dissonance, and, ultimately, victorious empowerment. Her fan base who follow her private life are given further incentive to listen to her music and learn more about her relationships and breakups. Additionally, some of her former partners also wrote songs about the breakups she publicized. Because they are associated with her, they also sell well. Who would have thought that breaking up could be such a powerful career move?

Swift also made the decision to break up with another partner: music streaming service Spotify. As a result, her new *1989* album was the first album to go platinum in 2014, with 1.287 million sold in its first week. This is an incredible feat; it is now the most successful record debut since 2002. Her breakups, or more precisely Taylor Swift's ability to win from her breakups, can be a case study for women around the world who have been fed the idea that romantic relationships are our ultimate reward, the triumphant end to a woman's life. Taylor's economic and cultural capitalization on a "breakup" can be an interesting symbolic tool for those who are still entrenched in the confining traditional roles of gender that keep them from moving forward.

Women have progressed an incredibly long way from the traditions of the baby boomer generation in which I was raised. My mother and the women of her generation living in Asia did not have the social atmosphere or opposing role model to challenge the patriarchal culture, practices, and internalized oppressions felt by many like her at the time. My mother's generation would not have been able to capitalize from challenging the obedience to men that was so heavily entrenched in the Confucian philosophy embedded in East Asian lifestyle and culture.

In all cultures, women continue to grapple with the challenges of breaking away from traditional upbringings, culture, and religion, much of which is used to keep women subordinated and subjugated. In such an environment, it is hard to simply "break up" and move on. Clearly, the broken relationships of Taylor Swift were not schemes for lucrative gain, but her music's clear inclusion of personal relationships and breakups exhibits that she is not someone who separates intimate life experiences and highly public art—she does not shy away from baring details that some women in previous times wouldn't have dared share. Whether this is something you agree with or not, she understands her influential place as a public figure—a mainstream one at that—and uses her music to relay parts of her life that would give similar power to her young, global, and largely female fan base.

Women who live in abusive families, abusive relationships, and hurtful situations would do well to consider carefully the possibility of a breakup. Women who are in domestic relationship often have such a difficult time leaving because of their inability to recognize they are in an abusive relationship. It is one of the most distorting and confining headspaces to be in because normally you are the only person stopping yourself from leaving. The Domestic Violence Intervention Program of Iowa is just one of several organizations that address domestic violence, reporting that women are significantly more likely to be killed in the two weeks after leaving than at any other time during the relationship. Women in abusive situations should be harnessed with the care and support of their social community, service providers, and law enforcement.

If there is one thing to glean from Swift's public prowess, it is that breakups can be the very antithesis of dissolution. They can bring the fruitful opportunities of unplanned change and the rawness of lived experience for greater creative ingenuity. To leave a bad relationship can be one of the most self-constructive acts towards discovering what independence can offer; and to truly understand how to be a good partner, understanding yourself as an individual rather than a part of a whole is crucial to the relationship's health and endurance.

It takes immense psychological work and careful external planning to leave abusive relationships, particularly if they are long-term and if children are involved. So, as a community, we need to create the resources to provide support for women who are in difficult relationships—even if they are not abusive. We should be more apt to recognize when our sisters are suffering in relationships rather than thriving. We need to stop associating breakups with failure and regard them as just another step in a new direction. Breaking up should not be seen as an end, but rather, a beginning.

Reflection

1. God wants us all to be in loving relationships. How can we work towards building healthy and loving relationships? What are some of the steps in maintaining such relationships?

2. Abuse is not part of God's strategy and plan. How can we rebuild broken relationships? What important steps can we take as Christians to heal and bring healing to our broken lives and communities?

UNCOVERING BILL COSBY'S FEET OF CLAY

> Or do you not know that your body is a temple of the Holy Spirit within you, which you have from God, and that you are not your own? For you were bought with a price; therefore glorify God in your body.
>
> *—1 Corinthians 6:19–20*

I grew up watching *The Cosby Show*. To say that it had an influence in my life would be an understatement. I used to build my days around it, bringing all my homework and food around the TV so I didn't have to get up during the run-time. I drew in extra close in front of the screen, wistfully dreaming about a perfect life with the Huxtables as my gregarious family—especially a dad like Cliff. He seemed to represent an idealized antithesis to how I saw my father at the time: easy-going, witty, sociable, and charming. The reach of *The Cosby Show* seemed apparent when I used to introduce my oldest son, Theodore. Nearly everyone my age assume I named him after Theo Huxtable, so suffice it to say, Bill Cosby left a deep influence on my generation and the culture of my adolescence.

When I read the long-unknown rape and sexual assault allegations against Bill Cosby, like many people, I just couldn't believe it—I was alarmed/agitated/angry and deeply disturbed. For many of us it seems as though our childhood icons are childhood friends, and Bill Cosby was akin to my alternative American TV dad. Now I see that this very veil of admiration, prestige, and familiarity was exactly what he used to take advantage of women. After so many allegations against numerous public figures, we can gain a better understanding of why it took so long for the system to support the allegations of these women whose cases were long uninvestigated.

Fifty-five women in total came forward against Cosby, and it was certainly time to hear their stories and fully investigate their claims. This is significant because Bill Cosby's story is not an isolated case. A growing number of men with varying degrees of power, influence, or wealth have been convicted or accused of committing sexual acts towards women and men in lesser positions of power. When allegations of rape and sexual violation are made against powerful, respected men, it seems that often their work and public persona overshadow the very allegations made against them and the very women who have suffered at the hands of such "significance." We can only discourage similar acts by others if the power of celebrity does not shield a person against criminal prosecution. Current culture reveres celebrity as much as it loathes it. We easily follow and accept certain celebrities as our role models, social pariahs, and scapegoats, or even our relatable kin. What many of us fail to recognize in our romanticization of celebrities is that many have "feet of clay," meaning they have major character flaws that are often overlooked or minimized in shadow of their public persona. Thus, it is no surprise that people feel such an uncomfortable disconnect between the constructed understanding of a person and the actual conflicting realities.

A person's image and the public's inclination to hold onto the respectable, known version of them has now been shattered by the disillusionment of the #MeToo movement—but there is still much work to be done. As we recognize the legal benefits of affluence, fame, and power, we must work towards uncovering the stories of those who were exploited by the power dynamics across all industries and support the pursuit of truth for those who have been affected.

This makes me ever more conscious as the mother of a young daughter who grew up dancing and performing. I am constantly aware of "spectators." This doesn't have to always relate to her on stage, but I know that girls who have been disciplined to execute perfection in performance are also those eager to please others, particularly authority figures, at their own expense. They may unknowingly fall into the oppressive trap of always doing as they are asked. In this sense, we should not simply teach our children to obey authority, but rather, to morally consider each difficult situation and develop their own mature sense of judgment.

Religion has a long history of justifying the submission of women, which has led to an affirmed, and even justified, culture of sexual oppression of women. We need to continuously address this patriarchal aspect of Christianity and aim towards its dismantling. When we address such issues of Cosby's allegations, we are trying to address the subordination of women that has been institutionally upheld, and the need to eliminate such injustices within our society strongly resonates within the church body.

In a society that continues to shame and blame our victims, it is crucial to teach our sons and daughters their role in supporting one another while combatting the powers of negative social influence. We need to ask ourselves how much longer we can tolerate the ways in which our social systems normalize, conceal, and support select individuals with social and economic power who exploit those who are more vulnerable than them. We cannot continue to allow women to be valued, treated, and seen as mere sexual victims who create unrest to the disadvantage of men. We need to take their allegations seriously in a changing landscape of deep social change in regard to gender and sexuality, where men feel as though they are being unrightfully persecuted because women finally are demanding to be heard.

We all need to express our demand for change. We need to encourage challenging dialogue to shift our culture away from one where men and women are held to different standards and move towards one that is egalitarian. The culture is changing and sex culture has to change with it. Consent has to be taught and respected as a necessary cue for further engagement. We need to support those who come forward and ensure that their allegations are fully, fairly, and transparently investigated. When appropriate, adjudication and punishment must follow.

Power, privilege, and prestige provide no exception to how we treat one another. They should not provide protection when allegations are made, nor should they discount the legitimacy of the victim's experience. Each of us is entitled to safety, respect, and dignity. We are all the equals. We are all God's children.

Reflection

1. The church needs to be a safe place to protect people from abuse; however, the church has often been a place of abuse and misuse of power. How can the church work out the existing abuses and also work towards a church that no longer harbors abuse?

2. Our body is the temple of the Holy Spirit. How do we take care of and nurture our bodies?

COUNT YOUR LOSSES

And when he comes home, he calls together
his friends and neighbors, saying to them, "Rejoice with
me, for I have found my sheep that was lost."

—Luke 15:6

I often daydream about finding everything I have ever lost. I think about entering my childhood bedroom and finding my whole life stashed in one towering mass. At the doorway are my baby teeth. Deeper in at the very bottom of the pile are old toys, mittens, socks, and school office candy; going up the pile are high-school diaries, hair ties, books, purses, clothes; heading farther up are reflective surfaces of money, sunglasses, and lipsticks; and at the very top of it all is a small gleaming light, a diamond: my engagement ring.

I have lost many things in my life but losing my engagement ring was one of the most distressing losses I have experienced. I remember contemplating for some time with my husband if it was even worth purchasing a ring, apprehensive because I was already going to have an expensive wedding ring. At the time, I didn't know what I wanted or how long it would be until we married, so I was anxious about making any wrong move in the life we set out to plan together. I questioned how marriage would change me, as I was still a student, struggling with work, my studies, and my finances. A diamond engagement ring would just be unnecessary; maybe we could go on a nicer honeymoon with that money instead. And then I received it.

There was no going back once I received the ring, not a question of costs or honeymoons, but to whom I would show it off first. I wore it and adored it, gushing at it on my hand, thinking of how I never imagined myself to be at that stage in my life where I wore an engagement ring before being wed. I rarely wore it in terror that I might misplace it—and when I lost it years later I felt mortification and regret that ate away at me for years. It still eats at me today when I think about it. I look back and think that I just didn't search hard enough or long enough. It was just a ring, but it was also a symbolic investment: an emblem of two young people promising their lives away to each other. Losing the ring was like saying goodbye to a moment of my life flushed with excitement, fear, and rampant possibility. After that loss, I decided to buy only fake rings. Diamond rings are just too easy to lose.

Then I lost my child in Las Vegas.

Looking back, it was not the best choice for a family vacation. Las Vegas isn't exactly the most family friendly place to visit with three young children. Nonetheless, we tried to make the most of it. We visited many wonderfully opulent, flamboyant hotels, one of the most enjoyable being the Circus Hotel. They had a whole floor dedicated for children equipped with a live theatre, whimsical attractions, animatronics, and a brand-new arcade. It was heaven for them. As my children went off to enjoy themselves with my husband, I went to the restroom. When I returned, my youngest, who was seven at the time, was suddenly gone. I know that any parent can relate to the panic of losing their child in a public space. The world simply stops turning, everything around you freezes, and all you do is call out and watch for their face to emerge from the distance.

Still in panic, my husband and I frantically asked a security guard for help; but he could not put the building on lockdown. We continued searching. I roamed around the never-ending arcade and started to get lost myself. All the games started looking the same, and I stopped moving to gain a sense of direction. When I stopped, something caught the corner of my eye. A white sheep moving around on a game screen. It bounced around in an open field, directionless. I thought of my son, the lost sheep.

One of Jesus' parables is that of the lost sheep. In the Gospels of Matthew and Luke, Jesus shares a story about a shepherd who leaves his flock of ninety-nine sheep in hopes of finding the one that was lost. Jesus shares this parable after religious leaders criticize him for eating with sinners. The story is an analogy of Jesus as the Shepherd, losing, searching, and rejoicing with people who are being found.

I ruminated on this parable in the midst of searching for my son: thinking about all the material things I had lost in my life and remembering how I too had been lost as a girl several times throughout my childhood. Before this experience, when I heard this story I thought that the shepherd should simply count his losses and move on. After all, he still had ninety-nine sheep, what would it matter? I had two other children. But in this context, I could not count my losses and move on—my lost child was more than me, he was everything. I had to do what I could to find my child.

We belong to Jesus. Jesus doesn't give up on us. Jesus searches for us when we get lost, when we find ourselves in the wilderness, and when we go through the dark night of the soul.

After thirty minutes or so, the security guard finally brought us to an arcade game on the opposite side of the room, where my son was curled up on the floor underneath one of the machines taking a nap after watching too many videos games. As any parent can imagine, the wave of relief that washed over me was unparalleled.

As I reflected on Jesus' parable, I realized that my search lasted less than an hour. Jesus continues to search to find the lost for as long as we exist. We all belong to God, thus, the lost one is worth searching for. This gives us hope.

The rejoicing of the shepherd upon finding the lost sheep is akin to God rejoicing when God finds us. The image of God rejoicing for the found and saved sinners explains why Jesus Christ ate with them. Each and every one of them was indispensable; each and every one of them worth saving. That is why he came to find and save the lost sheep of humanity.

We are part of Jesus' fold, his family. We mean too much to Jesus for Jesus to forget about us. During our most difficult times, we need to remember that Jesus will not give up on us. This assurance of God's love for us gives us a deep sense of hope and peace.

Reflection

1. When have you lost things? How did you search for them? What happened?

2. When have you been lost? Who searched for you? What happened when you were found?

3. How have you experienced the deep love from God that surpasses all understanding?

LONGING FOR PEACE

Peace I leave with you; my peace I give to you.
I do not give to you as the world gives. Do not let your
hearts be troubled, and do not let them be afraid.

—John 14:27

Being born in South Korea at the end of the sixties meant that I was born soon after the generation that had endured the Korean War. The country was steeped in the fresh remains of tragedy from a mere decade before, creating a new generation that had to rapidly reconstruct a new identity for the divided South Korea. Growing up in this time, I was raised not just to be afraid of our neighbor, North Korea, but to be hateful toward them. All that was associated with North Korea was regarded as a part of its evil, malicious, and unforgiving communist government. But one cannot live in fear. Fear begins as a small seed, sprouting and growing into a polluting entity that contaminates the surrounding ecosystem until it takes over completely. Fear is ruinous. It debilitates both our minds and our spirits. Furthermore, it is not Christian. Hence, I try to live a different way. I have tried to live out my faith by connecting with the Korean neighbor I was primed to contest.

Since my family and I emigrated to Canada in the early 1970s, I have returned to South Korea a total of six times. With every trip, I have gone to the 38th parallel, the border that divides North and South Korea. On my fourth visit back, I took my two older children to the infamous border. It was important to me that they understand not only their cultural roots but also the enduring problems of our motherland's history. The border is highly militarized, with countless South and North Korean soldiers, warnings, codes of conduct, and surveillance equipment stationed on every square inch of the perimeter. But during the visit with my children, I was also struck by its startling beauty. While punctuated with heavy metallic militarization, the surrounding land was lush, filled with dense greenery blanketed in a haze of cool, low-hanging mist. I marveled at how a site created from the horrors of human conflict and one of the world's most tyrannical dictatorships could be so striking. I looked out into the calm of forest and started to wonder whether my judgment had also been clouded by something in the hazy air.

In the summer of 2018, I traveled to South Korea as part of a delegation working for peace on the divided peninsula. While there, we met with the National Council of Churches in Korea and other prominent church leaders, members of the National Assembly, Speaker Moon Hee-sang, members of the Minjung Party, and the U.S. Ambassador to South Korea, Harry Harris. This particular visit to the 38th parallel brought new heartache. The demilitarized zone, or DMZ, is a reminder that regardless of time gone by, the loss of the division is irreparable. Under the Trump administration, I felt the reopening of past wounds and new anxieties for the North Korean people, as they re-encounter American forces that are far more volatile and confrontational than the previous.

At three inter-Korean summits in 2018, South Korean President Moon Jae-in and the North Korean leader, Kim Jong Un, met to discuss peace, trade, the denuclearization of the peninsula, and the ultimate objective of reunification. In discussion, the reunified Korea would allow easy and accessible travel across the border, allowing for families that have been separated for generations to finally come together once again. There have been some encouraging signs of progress from the recent discussions, but there are also signs of a continuing cycle of fear.

In an unprecedented summit in June 2018, President Trump and Kim Jong Un agreed to work toward denuclearization of the Korean Peninsula. Trump has touted making progress in denuclearization, but talks have been stalled by Kim's insistence on the removal of international sanctions as a precondition, and unhappiness with the United States' "nuclear umbrella" over South Korea. In late December 2018, North Korea reasserted its resolve not to denuclearize until the United States eliminates its own nuclear arsenal in the region. Further, Kim Jong Un asked that the United States significantly reduce its number of American troops—currently 28,500—stationed in South Korea.

If peace is ever to be obtained in the Korean Peninsula, the paths towards more talks, diplomacy, and shared interests must continue to be encouraged and developed. We cannot allow setbacks to derail any peace talks. More summits need to occur between the United States and North Korea so that mutual trust can be built, long-standing conflict can be healed, and peace can finally be obtained on the peninsula.

Christians must hold their ground as peacemakers in the face of disruptive world events and divisive leaders. Loving and embracing one another is a central principle of our faith. Jesus said, "Blessed are the peacemakers, for they will be called children of God" (Matthew 5:9). We look to North Korea as an example that, as participants in this collective journey for greater unity, we must make difficult decisions and steadfast efforts toward building agreement and trust with those whom we regard as the opposition. When that happens, I hope to one day return to a new Korea, one that I can take my children to and tell them, at the spot that was once the border, that hope can not only move people, but lands.

Reflection

1. What does it mean to live in hope, especially in times of fear and war?

2. What gives us hope to confront our relationship with the other?

3. How do we offer hope to others, especially when one feels hopeless?

SEEING MYSELF IN THE EYES OF A NORTH KOREAN

Let mutual love continue. Do not neglect to show
hospitality to strangers, for by doing that some have
entertained angels without knowing it.

—Hebrews 13:1–2

Some time after settling into Canada, I began to attend Korean school and Korean church in my early childhood. There, all the previous immediate fear of the North was only further reinforced, as I continued to be taught the same ideologies regarding North Koreans: that they are less than, immoral, and inhumane, and, most significantly, that they should not be regarded as human beings. South Koreans then frequently called them "bal-geng-i," meaning "Commies." I learned through the steady teaching and fearful rhetoric that despite not knowing what "Commies" or Communism was, the terms denoted them as a class of devilish beings, not even close to being what I was or what my parents were. While I certainly outgrew this perception, the seed was planted, and something in me always unconsciously thought of them as a subset of the world's most pitiful and inhuman.

Fast forward to 2014. In the beginning of that year, I began working with the Rev. Jesse Jackson for the release of Kenneth Bae, a Korean American who was being held prisoner in North Korea. We worked with Bae's family and government officials to try to secure his release. As our work progressed, we were able to secure a meeting with Jang Il Hun, ambassador of the Permanent Mission of the Democratic People's Republic of Korea to the United Nations.

After my initial excitement about the meeting, I began to think about the pragmatics of the situation, and fear took complete hold of me. It wasn't the mere residue of childhood fear, but a numbing fear that had been fed and shaped by all the events that had transpired since my adolescence. All the American rhetoric that had been prompted in news media against North Korea was political noise to the background of my childhood, and some way or another, the indoctrination had been laid and set.

For weeks before our meeting with Ambassador Jang in New York, I had tremendous, debilitating fear. I had one particular irrational fear based on an idea from Korean Church as a kid that North Koreans would come to my home and kidnap me. I went through countless scenarios in my head about the potential consequences of the confrontation. The North Koreans now had my phone number and could easily find my other personal information: my phone, my banking information, my home address. I feared they would find my location and the locations of all my family and friends; they would come for us in the middle of the night, and my loved ones would be accosted by North Korean officials who would take their lives all on my account.

When the day of the meeting came, I began to shake uncontrollably from the early morning. In the car ride up to the building I started to hyperventilate. I went over it in my head again and again, thinking of telling the driver to turn around, thinking of my family and regretting the moment I agreed to participate. When I reached the destination, I sat still in my seat for several minutes. It was one of those moments where I thought to myself, "this could be the beginning of the end." Finally, with great trepidation, I left the car, entered the building, and walked into the room where Ambassador Jang, the North Korean representative, was standing.

Our eyes met. In that moment, all the imagined terrors that had been circulating in my head subsided. As I looked at him, I saw my childhood best friend's father; I saw a narrow stature, with a focused, calm gaze spotlighted by an overhead light. I then saw my father; then my husband; then my sons—I saw something of myself. As I looked out to him, examining his visage, I saw a Korean everyman. I recognized myself in him, and whether we were enemies, neighbors, or friends, we were not all that different despite our strangely divergent circumstance—we were both created in the image of God.

I felt all my anxieties clear away as I sharpened my attention towards the ambassador, who was getting ready to speak.

What ensued was something I could never have imagined: a meaningful, hospitable discussion. No longer anchored by the dark weight of my preconceptions, I was able to speak openly with him and, most surprisingly, I was able to be sincere. During our discussion, we talked about North Korea, its people, and Kenneth Bae, who is a Korean American pastor in prison in North Korea. We exchanged good feelings, proposed changes, and even laughed together. Throughout the meeting, I kept asking myself, why were you so afraid?

North Americans are now in the same situation as I was before my meeting with Ambassador Jang. As Kim Jong Un reached out to President Trump to plan a summit and work toward a peace process, it was easy to be skeptical of Kim's intentions. We have been told time and time again that negotiating with North Korea is negotiating with evil and that we should never be so weak as to concede to their demands. We are afraid. And this fear, the fear of the other, immobilizes us. It also allows us to comfortably demonize those we do not know.

On July 27, 1953, the Korean Armistice Agreement was signed to cease fire between military forces, but it was not a peace treaty. The Korean War has never officially ended. Today more than 10 million families remain separated by the Demilitarized Zone at the 38th parallel in Korea. Many family members fled to the South, expecting to return back North in a few months. That never happened.

Family members are still separated, longing to see each other and be united—those of the older generations hope unification might happen in their lifetime. Conversely, while many members of the younger Korean generation are for the unification, the concern of its impact on the exceedingly prominent and competitive economy of South Korea leads many to hesitate giving their unfettered support. Even with these worries, however, Koreans on the peninsula and in the diaspora yearn to become one nation again. The two Koreas inhabit the same people, the same language, the same past, and the same hope: peace.

But peace cannot be attained in fear. Fear stifles any clarity of thought or observation we may have, further maintaining the prejudice that damages all parties across generations. I experienced confronting my own prejudice as I prepared to meet with Ambassador Jang. It only took one look, a look that forced me to see inside myself rather than reflect externally, to see both of us as partnered reflections of God's unified love for the conflicted world. This moment was the beginning of a profoundly redefining conversation in my life. It proved to me that the act of embracing our neighbors is not a voluntary act of morality, but a required obligation to the Divine.

Reflection

1. Do you have fear towards another ethnic group of people who are different from yourself? What is causing this fear? How do we overcome this fear?

2. God created all peoples. How do we begin to love one another, especially those from whom we are so different?

BECKONING FOR PEACE
IN UNREST

Pursue peace with everyone, and the holiness
without which no one will see the Lord.

—Hebrews 12:14

The teenage years are an emotionally volatile time in anyone's life. With a radical influx of new physical, psychological, and circumstantial changes, teenagers pose countless challenges for any parent. Children transitioning from childhood to early adulthood are emotional, rebellious, and subject to inevitable pressures, often making them more resistant to communication with those outside their immediate social circles. I have to empathize with their emotions in this predicament.

The idea of "teenagers" was only created seventy years ago. Before the Second World War there was no category or market demographic dedicated to the period between childhood and adulthood; after being a child, you were simply a young adult. Teenagers one hundred years ago were the bearers of significant responsibility, often taking care of the family farm or domestic enterprises at age thirteen, training for gainful employment at seventeen, marrying before they were twenty, and then becoming both a parent and spouse by their early twenties. The difficulties of average American teenagers then were acute, based on the rigidity of conservative social norms and cultural expectations.

While teenagers now face ever more penetrative social norms and powerful expectations, they certainly have more choice and freedom of expression than when I was a teenager in the 1980s. Nonetheless, adolescence from both my time and my children's is tied to social evolution, saturated in a voyage for personal fulfillment and self-discovery where the impending idea of one's adult self is ceaselessly reshaped and redefined. Teens have to reconcile the differing social philosophies of their parents, their peers, their culture, and ultimately themselves.

Unlike the teenagers of the past, who had to deal with the governing forces of the family, religion, and contained culture, teenagers of the recent half century are in the crossfire of adapting social landscapes, moral standards, and discordant value systems through the increasingly connected, prevalent, and sophisticated media. These conditions clearly make for a restless, unpeaceful era in one's life. Teenagers now are pushed to mature faster and "find themselves" earlier—for better or for worse.

In many ways, becoming a believer and going through the teenage years are analogous. The teenager can be compared to the "teenaged" believer, someone who is in the beginning part of their journey to reach a standard of spiritual equilibrium. This period is crucial for their eventual adulthood, and all who carry on to become devoted Christians certainly endure this passage of instability and conflict.

Finding faith today, for a person of any age, is becoming a much more challenging process. It is easy for individuals to become dis - illusioned when "spiritual parents" do not provide a competent example of maturity. There are so many other belief systems, activities, distractions, and deterrents in the modern age to keep people away from finding spiritual maturity. They turn to other things to find inner peace and fulfillment when the only thing that could push them in the right direction would be our guiding hand towards God.

Teenagers born after the mid 1990s, Generation Z, are being reared to quickly mature against the backdrop of the ecological crisis and the connection of social media. Their parents' generation, like ours and theirs before, are in either ignorance or denial, or are at odds with the issues that will affect their children in their adulthood for which they take little accountability. It could be this general ambivalence from those who are supposed to be their role models and the lack of moral integrity and decisiveness that have forced our young ones to take responsibility for their predecessor's mistakes and grow prematurely. Rather than dismissing the inevitable confusion of this young generation, we should be mobilized by them, imbue our faith onto them, and do what we can to shape them and the world for the better.

Dominant culture always looks towards our youth to see where we are headed as a society. So today, we look towards these young people with hope for a world that is handled with altruism and greater unity.

We have people like Greta Thunberg, the Swedish teen whose early solitary campaigns against climate change brought the world's attention towards the plight of the next generation's future. She began at age fifteen, spending her school days in front of the Swedish Parliament calling for stronger, swifter action on global warming. From this start, she began a student movement in other communities, and student strikes began taking place everywhere around the world after she addressed the 2018 Climate Change Conference held by the UN. Her abrupt prominence in the public eye, mainstream media, and public discourse has made her both an icon for the movement, a leader of her generation, and a major target. She has awoken the people in power, her parent's generation, making them finally acknowledge how little they have done to combat the environmental crisis that occurs faster and more violently. We have hope from this young generation—the children and the teenagers—who are already making global change in the midst of their own tumultuous changes in this period of their lives.

As I reflect on the remarkable stories of young people today, I think of my three children, who continue to grow into adulthood. They give me assurance that their full embarkment on their personal, spiritual, and life path will be fruitful and contribute to a greater cause. I can only hope that I do what I can do as an adult and as a role model to better guide them to lead their generation. Because today, teenagers bear a different responsibility from those of the past. They carry the weight of the world: the well-being of their planet and the endurance of life on earth. We adults need to be the best we can be, if not for ourselves, then for the people of the next generation. We must weaponize them with security in compassion, faith, and love, for a brighter today and a hopeful tomorrow.

Reflection

1. Do you know of teenagers who are changing the world? What are they doing?

2. How can you participate in building peace and saving the planet as you witness some younger teens and students are engaged in doing?

3. What are some of the biggest challenges to building and working towards peace in our world today?

FINAL THOUGHTS

In this parting, after you turn the page, close the book, return to life, shut your lids for a night's rest, and feel darkness swathe all around, call out for something. Call out for love; call out for peace; call out for light; call out for mercy; call out for God. Reach out, not for the purpose of gaining something in return, but because the call itself is the gift. The admission, that professed desire you seek, is not about the reception of certainty, but about reaffirmation of hope.

Life becomes the most meaningful it can be when you find gratitude for all you experience: the joy, the agony, the love, and the loss that we bear. We are reminded that in the chasm of intense beauty and suffering that we face daily, we are still alive, and that through feeling these heights of emotional and physical pain, we are the lucky ones—the blessed ones—to have lived through it.

However lost or isolated we feel in this physical world, remember that we are also tied to another one that lies beyond the shore of life, into the infinite waters of the afterlife. In the introduction of this book, I discussed hope as an anchor. The anchor is a symbol of stability sunken in the shore of our finite lives leading to the waters of our eternal ones. Then I posed a question: where do your anchors lie?

As we moved through this book reflecting upon various social, theological, and environmental issues, I sought to base the grandiosity of hope in the diverse plights of the real world. Perfect flashes of what this book could be stirred in my mind. I had intermittent fantasies for what I wanted it to become and what I could put out into the world with a sense of pride. I know that all of us share the same feeling for differing dreams. For most of us, the ambitions that we forge and redefine through time are what keep us going and also what keep us up at night, leaving us stagnant and unable to find peaceful rest. These dreams are important and often bring us a crucial sense of structure, direction, theme, or purpose to our lives. I believe in dreaming, but I also believe we must be wary of it. I say this because dreams carry us away. We become elated with our ideas for ourselves and each other, yet, when we wake from them, we find ourselves in the same place as when we lay down. We find ourselves blindly dropping our anchors away from the precipice of shore and on the thin surface of the midland, drifting and lolling out on ground. Thus, we find that dreams often make us complacent. Dreams can do the opposite of what they are intended to do, allowing us to aspire rather than to achieve.

This is why we hope.

Hope is our growing commitment to faith, and faith challenges us to remain certain despite uncertain circumstance. Hope is what sustains us and strengthens our spirits of shared humanity. Hope is what I intended to impart in this book and impart in my life.

If there is one thing I have learned in basing this book on hope in the real world, it is that hoping is not about being the beneficiary of good fortune but about putting desire into action. Hope requires us to be the agents in our own fates and anticipations before this life comes to an end. It denies us the time to sit back and wait; it denies us dreaming and instead calls for truth. Because to hope is not to dream, it is to live.

To live in hope, we must reconcile with our moral obligations and act upon them. We must make the world around us—the physical and the imagined, the logical and inexplicable, the present and the future—one that is more compassionate and just for all who come to pass through it.

We are a part of this one world, this chaotic, kaleidoscope of breathtaking life, change, and death—a place limited only by its own mortality. Our lives and the lives of those around us ebb and flow on a sailing boat with the illusion of spontaneity, but we are ultimately directed to the same place at the end of the journey. While we remain on the boat as we live, far from the shore we unfetter our anchor and cast out our hope, guiding it onto shore to be fixed onto the holy place thereafter. Thus, while we are here, let us hope not for the world of our dreams but for the world in which we live: the world of tomorrow and the world of today.

We must have one another in mind. We need each other. With solidarity, we can cultivate better lives for those who suffer around us and for the life and planet that suffers because of us. With this hope, we can liberate ourselves and move away from the darkness, the past, and even the present.

As we live in a time where ecological disaster can destroy the earth and all creation, we seek God and God's face in all things. As we seek the Divine, we gain a glimpse of hope.

Reside forever in hope. Let it become a way of seeing, breathing, living, and thriving. Let it call upon you, and may you call upon it, forming the ever-moving, unbreakable connection between you, faith, the world, and God.

AFTERWORD

Reformed Christians often neglect the spiritual traditions within their own heritage and, as a result, they are often inclined to make false distinctions between the pursuit of justice and the practice of spirituality. I have heard friends and colleagues dismiss the importance of spiritual disciplines because they focused too much on the voice within as opposed to listening to the larger community. Others have argued that Reformed Christians should adopt the term piety rather than spirituality to reflect John Calvin's description of the attitudes and practices that give shape to the Christian life. Some, who are committed activists and advocates, express an "allergy" to the term spirituality altogether and see the pursuit of justice as distinct from spiritual practices. However, I do not think that spirituality and the pursuit of justice can be so easily compartmentalized and placed into neat, clearly defined categories.

Spiritual disciplines create the space and time to steady yourself in hope and ground your actions in the awareness of your own place within God's creative activity. Howard Thurman, the great social mystic and co-founder of the Church of Fellowship for All Peoples, suggests that "social action . . . is an expression of resistance to whatever tends to, or separates one from, the experience of God, who is the very ground of [our] being."[4] Our Christian hope emerges from the awareness of our deep connection to God, others, and the planet upon which we depend for sustenance.

Grace Ji-Sun Kim provides a model for us in this devotional guide of ways to take up challenging questions of peace, justice, love, and resistance in a society driven by values of individualism, self-sufficiency, efficiency, productivity, and independence. She lifts the present context into the light of God through biblical stories, adept theological thought, and reflective prayer questions. Throughout *Hope in Disarray*, Grace welcomes friends to express positions long ignored, as they find challenging and complex meaning in the total interdependence of all of life. We cannot help but to listen and join them in their efforts to make positive change in the world.

Meditation, silent retreat, daily examen, and development of a daily rule are additional practices that sustain us in these efforts and invite us to see beyond the limitations of human imaginations formed and framed by our roles, social class, gender identity, cultures, institutions, and faiths. Spiritual disciplines invite us to live in God's imagination and to situate our efforts in relation to a much a larger web of life and vision for the world. In this way, the pursuit of social justice is never an end of and for itself, but an expression of the reality that our interdependence reflects a Unity and Love that connects us and the greater world. May we live with the plight to see justice in our world of disarray, and live through God's imagi - nation, our spiritual home, to forever abide in hope.

Rev. Dr. Elizabeth Hinson-Hasty
Bellarmine University

4. Howard Thurman, "Mysticism and Social Action," *A.M.E. Zion Quarterly Review* Vol. 92, No. 3 (October 1980): 9.

ABOUT THE AUTHOR

GRACE JI-SUN KIM, an ordained minister of word and sacrament within the Presbyterian Church (USA), is professor of Theology at Earlham School of Religion. She is the author or editor of nineteen books, most recently *Hope in Disarray: Piecing Our Lives Together in Faith*, *Reimagining Spirit*, and *Keeping Hope Alive*. *Reimagining Spirit* was listed as one of the Englewood Review of Books' Best Theology Books of 2019 and *Intersectional Theology*, co-written with Susan Shaw, as one of the Best Theology Books of 2018. Kim is honored to be included in Englewood's list of "Ten Important Women Theologians That You Should Be Reading" and their list of books to read under "Our God Is Too White? Diversifying Our Theology."

Kim has served on the Board of Directors for the American Academy of Religion (AAR) and AAR's Research Grants Jury Committee, and was co-chair of AAR's steering committee, Women of Color Scholarship, Teaching and Activism Group. She is married to Dr. Perry Y. C. Lee, and they have three children, Theodore, Elisabeth, and Joshua.